TREASURED

Polish

RECIPES

FOR AMERICANS

by

POLANIE CLUB

POLANIE EDITORIAL STAFF

Marie Sokolowski and Irene Jasinski, Co-Chairmen

Josepha Contoski
Virginia Fitzsimons
Victoria Janda
Lucille Jasinski

Monica Krawczyk
Alina Polzak
Maria Smorczewska-Bullis

Illustrated by Stanley Legun

Cover Design by Marya Werten

ALLEGRO
EDITIONS

CONTENTS

DEDICATED TO

Our American friends who in the enjoyment
of Polish foods encouraged us to publish the
recipes and to the countless number of American cooks of Polish ancestry who remember
Mother's and Grandmother's foods with nos-
talgia.

FOREWORD

This is no ordinary cook book. This is a cook book full of excellent Polish recipes, collected through the years by a group of Polish American ladies.

Anyone who has lived in Poland knows that Polish cooking is delicious. Its typical dishes are reminiscent of the best French and central European cooking.

The famous soups, **zakąski** (hors d'oeuvres) and pastries cannot be excelled anywhere.

Every Polish woman has been taught the art of managing a household in the most economical way. Nothing is ever thrown away, and they have clever ways of using left-overs, such as making cordials of fruit skins, which are said to have medicinal qualities. This training has stood Polish women in good stead, now that they have lost everything. They earn their living working in restaurants, making pastries at home, cooking for orphanages and hospitals. Many little restaurants have opened up in small temporary wooden shacks built amongst the bombed-out houses and there one can buy very good cooked hams, pastries and other delicacies.

Looking back on years in Poland brings back many memories, not only of good food. These are bound to be poignant and saddened by the thought that such great changes have taken place. The houses in Warsaw we used to know are in ruins and most of the owners are scattered to the four corners of the earth, or dead.

Well do I remember the young Polish chef we employed in Warsaw, a man who could make anything from the most tasty roasts to delicate light-as-air pastry. Never, during the fifteen years I kept house and tasted the best food in many countries, have I seen such an artist in the culinary art.

He had been beautifully trained in the best Cordon Bleu cooking school in Warsaw and as a proof that he was quite exceptional, when Anthony Biddle came as American Ambassador to Poland several years before the war and was looking for the best cook for the Embassy, whom should he get but our friend whom we employed some years before!

Since the Biddles gave very fine parties in the handsome 18th century palace of Count Raczynski, as well as in the charming chateau **Natolin** they rented near Willanow twelve miles outside of Warsaw, our artist cook had an excellent opportunity to show off his skill.

When I arrived in Minneapolis just before the last war, almost my first friends were these ladies of Polish descent who have compiled this book.

We worked on Polish Relief together, and I find that they too have lived up to the warmhearted, traditional Polish hospitality and friendship.

I accepted with sincere appreciation their invitation to write this foreword, both to pay my tribute to the Polish people and to recommend this book, for I know the reader will find many treasures among its recipes.

MARGARET B. HAWKS

STANLEY LEGUN

INTRODUCTION

To the Pole the holiest of all edibles is bread. His petition in his daily prayer has a special meaning for him, for so many times the Pole has had to do without it. Famine and wars have been a common occurrence in the Old World. Therefore a Pole never wastes his bread. He eats the dark, heavier breads for his every day fare. His holiday baking calls for **piękna pszenna mąka, beautiful wheat flour**. Every crumb of old bread is used for food. Polish cooking requires the use of bread crumbs for binding, thickening, lining of baking pans, and garnish. Vegetables **Polonaise** are served with a thick coating of buttered bread crumbs. The bread is dried completely and put through a grinder. The crumbs may be kept indefinitely in a clean brown paper bag. They may be stored in a glass jar. The cover on the jar must be punctured to keep the crumbs from getting musty.

Baking in Poland, delicious in its results, was a test of endurance and muscle. Old recipes say "Beat butter or eggs and sugar for one hour, and in one direction only." We have not changed any of the ingredients in the recipes, but we have changed the manipulation. We have tried to bring it up to date with no sacrifice of quality. A hand-driven egg beater of the modern type can do in thirty minutes what a spoon did in sixty. And the electric-driven beater shortens the time to fifteen or twenty minutes and gives just as good results.

For best baking results all ingredients should be at room temperature, all other theories notwithstanding. In short pastry, too, it is the chilling after the dough is made that makes it flaky rather than the use of hard fat and ice water in the mixing. All flour should be warm and sifted before measuring. To intensify the yellow color in coffee cakes and other pastries, add the salt to the egg yolks.

All dough must be leavened. Air is the chief leaven. Air is beaten into egg whites. Creaming fat and sugar incorporates

9

some air into the mixture. Flour absorbs air when it is sifted. Air is beaten directly into the batter if it is of an elastic texture. The other three leavening agents used to cause carbon dioxide in a dough are: yeast, baking soda and baking powder. Yeast, the oldest of them, is widely used in Poland. Soda was used to some extent long before the invention of baking powder and many old cookbooks and family recipes specify its use. Baking powder is slowly being introduced.

The generous use of butter in the recipes may startle you. You may ask do they use so much butter in Poland? The answer is yes and let us tell you why. In the rural areas, every household owns a cow and many own herds of prize cattle. European refrigeration leaves much to be desired. Of necessity the Polish farmer kills his livestock in the cold months when meat will keep. Shortening or lard rendered in the cold months will not stand the summer's heat. The vegetable shortenings that keep well in or out of the ice-box were unknown to Europe until they began to arrive in food packages after the war. The farmer's faithful cows give milk all year. In almost no time at all, the farmer's wife can churn a jar of butter for her table and kitchen. Use your judgment in making substitution for butter but the flavor of it in foods is its own reward.

When purchasing butter in paraffined cartons, always remember that each quarter-pound print of butter measures exactly one-half cup. When you want to measure one-fourth cup of butter, just cut one of the quarter-pound prints in half. This saves measuring in a cup. Thus time is saved and butter, too, for in most instances it is impossible to remove all of the butter from the measuring cup.

Eggs are used abundantly. They are counted up to ten. After that they are measured. A recipe may call for a liter or **pół-kwaterek** (half-pint) or **kope** (sixty) eggs. Often the farmer's wife earns enough money from the sale of eggs from her chickens to run the household. There always are enough left for her use.

Not all American cooks know how to use sour cream and sour milk to advantage. For centuries European countries have recognized the beneficial qualities of sour cream, buttermilk and sour milk. Lactic acid in these foods is the result of the action of certain bacteria on milk sugar or lactose. This healthful food is of the greatest hygienic and therapeutic value to the digestive tract and health in general. Sour cream gives additional zest to soups, is the finest and most delicate marinating agent for meats, blends naturally with both garden and fruit salads, is delicious in desserts, and makes the tenderest of fine

10

textured cakes, cookies and bread stuffs. Its use in Poland is that of a necessary staple.

For baking purposes, regular sweet cream may be soured by adding two tablespoons of lemon juice or vinegar to one cup of cream and letting it stand for ten minutes. For all other uses of sour cream, get the commercial sour cream. It is a very thick product with a consistency more like mayonnaise than cream. It is sold in pint jars.

Onion, garlic and wine are the soul of good cooking, but garlic must be used with great discretion. When a recipe indicates "onions chopped fine," we mean **chopped fine** since a dish can be ruined if it is full of chunks of onion. An onion chopper does this perfectly in a wink. Sauteing in butter moderates the flavor.

The onion and all its relatives—leeks, chives, shallots and scallions are a food and seasoning in Poland. Dill with its fragrance of summer fields is chopped or cut fine and used to flavor many foods. Once you taste it, the flavor grows on you and lingers.

Polish cuisine with its hauntingly good flavors uses all spices but with a light touch. No foods are smothered with spices. It is better to use too little of any herb rather than too much. You gain the flavor of spice if you use a pepper mill or mortar and pestle to pound the whole spice to a fresh powder when recipe calls for ground spice.

For flavoring, get the vanilla bean if you can, in preference to the liquid. Immerse the bean in milk or liquid, letting the liquid absorb the flavor, remove bean and use liquid in pastry. Keep the bean in sugar in a cannister and use the flavored sugar in baking and for sprinkling.

The Polish table is attractively set. In season, not only is there a centerpiece of flowers but various leaves are arranged in mosaic patterns. The sides of the tablecloth are decorated with leaves in garland effects. This artistic ability is inherent in the people. No special training is available. Even the very modest homes in Poland were known for the careful serving of meals and the artistic arrangement of table settings.

In some homes table linens were heirlooms passed from grandmother to granddaughter, most of them imported from Holland and England. Later Polish linens, sheer and beautiful, with woven family crests or monograms made of Polish flax by the firm of **Żyrardów,** equalled the imported linens.

11

From early centuries Poland was an agricultural country, busy in its domestic pursuits. This way of living developed in the nation a discrimination in its choice of foods. Its climate favored the growth of nearly everything to make Poland self-sustaining. Only citrus and southern fruits, coffee, tea and spices were imported.

Warm hospitality is a characteristic of the nation. Stranger or friend is always welcome and never bid farewell without a serving of food—it little matters how modest—**Czem chata bogata, tem rada.** (The little cottage shares what it has). Bread and salt symbolize the mainstay of life. In Poland these symbols welcome guests and imply wishes of good fortune, good health, and a bountiful life.

With the people's love of good food, cooking was considered an art, to be learned by all, thoroughly and reverently. A daughter learned to cook from her mother. Well could the rhyme "can she bake a cherry pie?" have originated in Poland when some young man's fancy was turned by a girl. Not even the devastating wars destroyed all Polish cook books. These books were carefully kept from generation to generation. After the last war, among the first books to be published were cook books.

Polish cooking is versatile. Every district has its special dishes, like its own regional folk dress and customs.

Cooking can be a delightful occupation. We hope our recipes will help to make it a creative art in your home.

THE EDITORS

12

MEASUREMENTS

Throughout this book all measurements are level.

A small **t** indicates a **teaspoon.**

A capital **T** indicates a **tablespoon.**

All other abbreviations are in common usage. Since accurate measuring is essential to good cooking, use of commercial standard measuring cups and spoons is important. A coffee cup or soup spoon will hold the ingredient, but the variation in quantity will spoil the dish.

Nothing is said as to the number of servings which may be obtained from any given recipe. It is understood among cooks that unless a statement is made to the contrary, the accepted servings are **six.**

EQUIVALENTS

4 cups flour, 2 cups sugar, 2 cups butter....................1 pound

"Dash"..less than 1/8 teaspoon

3 teaspoons ....1 tablespoon

2 tablespoons ....1 fluid ounce

16 tablespoons ....1 cup

2 cups ....1 pint

2 pints ....1 quart

4 quarts ....1 gallon

1 wine glass..1/4 cup

Butter—1/4 lb......................................1/2 cup or 8 tablespoons

Cream, heavy, 1/2 pt. ....1 cup or 2 cups whipped

Dates—Pitted ....1 lb.—2 1/2 cups

Eggs, whole ....4-6—1 cup

Eggs, whole ....10—1 pound
Eggs—Yolks ....10-14—1 cup
Eggs, whites ....8-10—1 cup
Lemon—1 medium..............................3 tablespoons juice
Lemon—1 medium............................1½ teaspoons grated rind
Orange—1 medium..½ cup juice
Orange—1 medium..........................1 tablespoon grated rind
Marshmallows ....16—¼ pound
Nuts, in shells..1 lb.—3½ cups shelled
Nuts, shelled and chopped................................¼ lb.—1 cup
Potatoes..1 lb—3 medium size
Raisins..15 oz. package—3 cups
Rice..1 lb.—2 cups uncooked
Rice..1 lb.—6· cups cooked
Sugar—Granulated ....2 cups—1 pound
Sugar—Brown................................2⅔ cups— 1pound
Sugar—Powdered..3 cups—1 pound
Sugar—Loaf..116 squares—1 pound
Cornstarch....................1 tablespoon—2 tablespoons flour
Cocoa, 3½ tablespoons and ½ T butter—1 oz. or square
    chocolate
Sour milk, 2 tablespoons vinegar or lemon juice and sweet
    milk ....1 cup
American cheese........................5 cups grated—1 pound
Cream cheese................6⅔ tablespoons—1 3-oz. package
Graham crackers..........................9 coarsely crumbled—1 cup
Graham crackers..........................11 finely crumbled—1 cup
Salted crackers..........................7 coarsely crumbled—1 cup
Salted crackers..........................9 finely crumbled—1 cup
Vanilla wafers..........................22 coarsely crumbled—1 cup
Vanilla wafers..........................26 finely crumbled—1 cup
Zwieback....................................7 coarsely crumbled—1 cup
Zwieback....................................9 finely crumbled—1 cup
1 No. 1 can..1⅓ cups
1 No. 2 can ....2½ cups
1 No. 2½ can ....3½ cups
1 No. 3 can ....4 cups
Half pint whipping cream makes garnishes for 15 servings.
1 kilogram = 2¼ lbs.; about 450 grams/45 deko = 1 lb.;
about 100 grams/10 deko = 3 oz.; 1 liter = 1½ liquid qts.

14

EATING TIME IN POLAND

In the cities the average working hours are from seven in the morning to three-thirty o'clock in the afternoon. Breakfast is served at six-thirty, lunch, **drugie śniadanie,** at eleven o'clock, dinner at three-thirty or four o'clock in the afternoon and supper at seven-thirty o'clock in the evening. On the farms, the tillers of the soil eat their breakfast at sunrise, pack a lunch and eat in the field when they get hungry and return to their homes at sunset for supper.

A delightful Polish custom is the break in the afternoon routine for a visit to the many tea shops, **cukiernie.** This is done between the hours of three and six o'clock in the afternoon. If you order tea, it is brought to you in tall thin glasses. Sliced lemon with the tea is more popular than cream. Coffee is served in cups, topped with whipped cream.

The pastry accompaniments in the tea shop offer you an amazing array of choices. You may order a wedge of torte filled with a deliciously flavored nut filling with a subtle touch of rum. But more likely you will choose the individual pastries of which there are many and fascinating kinds. In Poland when a cake is baked in a sheet pan, the top is not frosted and then the cake served in squares. No, indeed, the cake is first cut into squares, rounds or rectangles and each piece gets its individual frostings and decorations. Pure fruit flavors and marmalades are used abundantly. You may prefer to order filled cream puffs, **pączki, chruścik, mazurek,** or any of the other many delicacies. Before you leave you will buy some of the attractively stocked sweet milk chocolate, fruit pastes and bon bons.

Another delightful custom is an evening spent on **pół-czarnej** (half black). The guests arrive at nine o'clock and are invited to the dining table which is spread with cold cuts of meat, rolls, tea cakes and fruit. The attentive host tends to your glass with your favorite liqueur. The hostess fills and refills your demitasse cup with strong black coffee. As the evening progresses, conversation flows freely and a spirit of hale comraderie prevails.

15

APPETIZERS
ZAKĄSKI

An unlimited variety of delectable bits called **Zakąski** are served to introduce the dinner. Their purpose is to stimulate the appetite but not to satisfy it. Since the appetite is first stimulated through the eye, special care is given to make the appearance of the appetizer attractive. The serving is simple. As a first course preceding dinner, they are arranged on service plates and passed in the living room with beverages or served at the table immediately after the guests are seated.

Suggestions:

Tomatoes marinated in oil	Pickled Mushrooms
Cold Meats	Cold Tongue
Caviar	Herring
Oysters	Cold Sliced Chicken
Anchovies	Shrimp
Cold and Smoked Fish	Olives
Stuffed Eggs	Pickled Onions
Cheese	Marinated Vegetables

In the dinner menu, appetizers are followed by soup, meat, oftentimes fish, potatoes, vegetables, both cooked and green, dessert and tea or coffee. At state and formal dinners, wines are served with each course.

Many Poles traditionally from generation to generation maintained private wine cellars. Correct serving of liquors was strictly observed in table etiquette. Cocktails were unknown. With canapes were served various whiskeys. The weaker kinds were for the ladies.

There was a favorite order of serving wines.
With oysters: White Rhine or White Burgundy.
After the soup: Spanish Wines, Marsala, Madeira or Port.
With fish: French wines, Chablis, Sauterne, Chateaux Lafite.
With roast meats: French wines, Bordeaux or light Hungarian wines.

16

With fruit ices at elaborate dinners: the French Latour-Blanche or Chateu D'Ygnem.

After pastries: Champagne.

With dessert: Old Tokay, Hungarian Maslarz, Malaga, and old Polish honey wines.

CANAPES
KANAPKI

Canapes are made on a foundation of bread. An unending variety of mixtures or ingredients may be used to cover the small squares or rounds of bread. These tasty tidbits and savory morsels are served often as appetizers before dinner and then again you will find them as refreshments at afternoon teas. They are always attractively arranged on large trays or platters—never crowded or heaped. They are finger foods, easily handled and made very small. Their variety and importance of appearance offer the hostess a wide scope for her creative ability.

We suggest:

Force cooked eggs through coarse sieve. Mix the white with a mite of finely cut greens of onion. Make a border of the yolk and season to taste.

Border cold chicken with colored aspic.

Cover the buttered bread with mustard or horseradish and serve cold ham or tongue.

Border caviar, salmon, anchovies with mayonnaise, chopped egg and green capers.

Cover small rounds of rye bread with pickled herring, onion, sour apple, chopped fine and tossed with 1 teaspoon of salad oil.

Force through coarse sieve chicken liver sauteed with mushrooms, lemon and onion juice, seasoned to taste.

Remove seed sections from small slices of tomato. Fill alternately with black caviar and riced cooked egg.

Border pickled onions with pickled beets forced through ricer. Sprinkle with olive oil and garnish with riced egg yolks.

Przez posły wilk nie tyje.

The wolf does not fatten on messengers.

SOUPS
ZUPY

Soup is an essential course in the dinner menu. Meat soup stocks have practically no nutritive value but are important because they stimulate the appetite and aid the digestion and are used as foundation in many soup recipes.

MEAT STOCK
Rosół

3 lbs. beef
Beef bone with marrow
3 qts. cold water
1 T salt
1 onion
1 cabbage leaf

1 celery stalk
2 sprigs parsley
 or small parsnip
2 carrots
1 bay leaf

Bring the meat, bone and water to a boil. Do not skim. Simmer slowly for one hour until no more scum gathers at the top. Remove from fire and add 1 tablespoon of cold water. This will bring the fat to the top. The fat is indigestible and should be removed. Add rest of ingredients and continue to cook slowly until the meat is tender. Time of cooking will depend on the cut and quality of meat. Strain soup and remove rest of fat. This makes 3 pints of stock.

In adding onion to soups for flavor, cut the stem and root end. Do not peel. Wash clean, cut lengthwise, and brown over open flame.

CHICKEN SOUP
Kurzy Rosół

3 to 4 lb. chicken
Chicken feet
Gizzard and heart
3 qts. water
Salt to taste

1 onion, browned
1 carrot
1 stalk celery
2 sprigs parsley

Cut chicken at joints. Scald and skin the feet and remove the nails. Extra chicken feet will enhance the flavor of the soup. If the flavor of the meat is to be retained, cover chicken with hot water. If you would rather save the flavor in the soup,

18

cover chicken with cold water. Bring to a boil and do not skim. Simmer for an hour, then add rest of ingredients. When chicken is tender, remove the meat from soup. Strain soup and remove the fat. Chicken may be cooked the day before. Cool soup after straining and set in refrigerator. Before serving, lift off the hard layer of fat from top and serve soup hot.

BARLEY SOUP
Krupnik

2 qts. meat stock
2 carrots, diced
1 stalk celery, chopped
2 potatoes, diced
Sour cream, optional

6 ozs. pearl barley
⅓ cup mushrooms
4 T butter
Salt and pepper

Wash the barley and cover with 1 cup meat stock. Bring to boiling point and simmer until tender. Add the butter gradually. In the remaining stock boil the vegetables and mushrooms. Then add the cooked barley and season with salt and pepper. Add a few tablespoons of sour cream, if you wish.

BARSHCH
Barszcz

The foundation of barszcz is **kwas,** the sour liquid obtained from fermented beets, and good meat stock.
Kwas

8 medium red beets
3 qts. lukewarm water

1 slice sour rye bread

Wash and peel beets, cut into thick slices and place in a stone or earthenware jar. Cover with lukewarm water. The process of fermentation may be hastened by placing the rye bread in the jar. Cover the jar to protect it from dust and keep in warm place. When the **kwas** is sour, pour it off the beets into bottles, seal and keep in the refrigerator. Add to the meat stock (page 18) sufficient **kwas** to give the desired sourness and let it just come to a boil. Overboiling or reheating fades the color. If the color is not beet red, grate a beet into a sieve and pour the soup through this into the tureen or soup bowls.

Barszcz is usually served in cups after the appetizers, together with small pasties, delicate sticks of flaky pastry. It is also served in soup plates with **uszka**—tiny squares of very thin noodle paste folded over a meat filling to form a triangle and the two ends pinched together, (page 31).

19

BARSHCH WITH CREAM
Barszcz Zabielany

Meat stock and beet **kwas**
1 cup sour cream
1 T flour

Make a smooth paste of the flour and sour cream. Bring meat stock and beet **kwas** to boiling point and quickly stir in the sour cream and flour mixture. Bring to boiling point again and serve. Hard-cooked eggs cut in quarters, small pieces of sausage or other meat are sometimes put into the soup tureen. You may add strips of the beet which has been cooked with the stock.

EASY BARSHCH
Łatwy Barszcz

12 medium beets	1 medium onion, sliced
1 qt. water	Juice of 1 lemon
1 T sugar	2 cups bouillon
Salt and pepper	

Wash and peel the beets. Cook beets and onion in water until beets are tender. Add juice of lemon, sugar, salt and pepper. Let stand over night. Strain. Add bouillon (made by using 2 bouillon cubes and 2 cups of hot water). Chill thoroughly and serve in cocktail glasses.

BEET GREEN SOUP
Barszcz Botwinkowy

2 qts. soup stock	1 T sugar
2 bunches fresh beet greens	1 T flour
2 T lemon juice	1 cup sour cream

Wash small beets and greens thoroughly. Cut fine, add to boiling meat stock, and cook for 10 minutes. Add the sugar. Blend flour with sour cream, adding 2 tablespoons of the hot soup stock. Stir into the soup and bring just to the boiling point. If you do not have sour cream, use sweet cream and lemon juice to flavor the soup. The soup stock may be made from pork cuts like spare ribs or neck bones. Then omit sugar. Serve with hot boiled potatoes and chopped meat from soup stock.

~~~~~~

Kęs chleba i swoboda.
A crust of bread and liberty.

VOLHYNIAN BEET SOUP
Barszcz Wołyński

6 medium beets	Sour rye bread crust
1 head cabbage	1 sour apple, chopped
4 large tomatoes	1/4 cup navy beans
Meat stock	Salt and pepper
2 T butter	

Soak the beans over night and cook until tender. Peel, slice and cook beets. Quarter the cabbage, scald in hot water. Wash, peel and smother in butter the tomatoes and force through coarse sieve. Add vegetables, beans and chopped sour apple to meat stock and cook for half hour. Put the rye bread crust into the soup and keep it there until it becomes very soft, but lift out before it falls apart. Pour the hot soup on plates and stir into each serving a tablespoon of sour cream.

TOMATO SOUP
Zupa Pomidorowa

1½ lbs. spare ribs	1 celery stalk
3 qts. cold water	1 parsley root
1 qt. or 2 lbs. tomatoes	Left-over vegetables
1 onion, browned	or vegetable juices
½ cup sour cream	1 T flour
Salt and pepper to taste	

Cook meat, vegetables and water slowly for one hour. Remove meat, strain soup and press through coarse sieve. Cool soup and set in refrigerator. Before serving, lift off the hard layer of fat from top. Bring soup to boiling point and add the flour blended with sour cream and bring to boiling point again. Serve with rice. This is a very substantial soup, almost a meal in itself.

Place spare ribs in baking pan, cover with your favorite sauce and bake in 350° oven for 1 hour.

SORREL SOUP
Zupa Szczawiowa

2 qts. meat stock	½ cup sour cream
1 lb. young fresh sorrel	4 T butter
1 or 2 small potatoes	4 egg yolks
Salt and pepper to taste	

Clean the sorrel and scald it. Chop fine, cook in butter until tender and rub through sieve. Boil the potatoes, rub them through sieve, and mix with sorrel puree. Season with salt and pepper. Simmer for 10 minutes. Beat the egg yolks and add to them 2 tablespoons of hot soup. Pour into simmering soup and heat to just below the boiling point. Add the sour cream and serve immediately.

PEA SOUP
Grochówka

1 ham bone	2 large onions
½ lb. split yellow peas	3 qts. water
¼ lb. split green peas	1 cup milk
2 stalks celery	1 T flour
1 sprig parsley	1 T butter

Cover ham bone with water and add the peas, celery and parsley. Simmer until peas are soft enough to put through sieve. Fry the onion in butter until slightly burned, add to soup and continue to simmer for half hour. Brown the flour lightly in butter and add to soup. Serve with grated cheese or croutons.

DILL PICKLE SOUP
Zupa Ogórkowa

3 large dill pickles	1 cup sour cream
3 T butter	2 T flour
Meat or vegetable stock	

Slice the pickles and saute in butter and flour until thoroughly wilted. Add the stock and simmer slowly for half hour. Strain and add the sour cream. Serve with **pierożki** (page 114).

LEMON SOUP
Zupa Cytrynowa

Meat stock	1 cup hot water
½ cup rice	Juice of 1 lemon
2 T butter	1 cup cream

Wash rice in cold water. Cook in double boiler in hot water and butter until very tender. Add cream and mix thoroughly. Add lemon juice and enough meat stock to serve 6 persons. Bring to boiling point and serve immediately. Garnish each plate with a thin slice of lemon.

DUCK SOUP
Czarnina

Fowl trimmings and blood	3 whole peppers
1½ lbs. spare ribs	10 dried prunes
1 stalk celery	Dried apples or pears
2 sprigs parsley	15 cherries or raisins
1 small onion	2 T flour
4 whole allspice	1 cup sweet cream
4 whole cloves	1 t sugar
Salt to taste	½ cup vinegar

Put vinegar into glass or crockery bowl (not metal) and into this catch the blood when killing the duck or goose and stir to avoid coagulation. Fresh pig's blood may also be used.

22

Cover the fowl trimmings and spare ribs with water, bring to boiling point and skim. Put spices, celery, onion and parsley into a sack and add to soup. Cook slowly until meat is almost done (about 2 hours). Remove spice sack, add fruit and cook for one-half hour more. Blend flour with ½ cup of the blood mixture, add 3 tablespoons of soup stock, and pour into soup, stirring constantly. Add sugar and cream and bring to boiling point. Serve with egg noodles or potato dumplings.

SAUERKRAUT SOUP
Kapuśniak

2 lbs. smoked pork shanks
   or pig's feet
1 qt. water
1 onion, well browned
1 qt. sauerkraut juice
¼ cup sugar
¼ cup cream
1 egg
1 T flour
¾ cup milk

Cook meat in water until well done. Add onion, sauerkraut juice and sugar. Beat egg, add flour, milk and cream. Add to soup and bring to boiling point. Serve with potato dumplings.

EASTER SOUP
Żurek Wielkanocny

2 cups oatmeal
2 cups warm water
Crust of sour rye bread

Polish sausage and water
1 T horseradish
Salt to taste

Mix oatmeal with water and add the bread. Let stand at least 24 hours until it sours. Strain. Cook sausage in water for one hour. Remove sausage and skim the fat accumulated in the water. Add liquid to the oatmeal mixture. Mix in a tablespoon of horseradish. Serve hot with slices of Polish sausage and hard-cooked egg, boiled potatoes or croutons. Serves 6.

You may prefer to make this soup an easier way. Cover the sausage with 2 quarts of water and cook for 1 hour. Remove sausage, cool water and set in refrigerator over night. The next day remove the fat, salt to taste, add 2 tablespoons vinegar or lemon juice, 1 tablespon horseradish and thicken with 2 tablespoons flour mixed with 1 cup sweet cream. Bring to boiling point and serve hot as above.

Mędrsze jaja od kury.
Wiser the eggs than the hen.

MEATLESS SOUPS
ZUPY POSTNE

VEGETABLE STOCK
Postna Zupa

2 qts. cold water
4 carrots
4 stalks celery
Salt and pepper

1 onion
2 sprigs parsley
2 T butter

Wash vegetables, cut into small pieces and saute in butter under cover until they turn yellow. Add water and simmer for half hour. Strain before serving.

MUSHROOM SOUP WITH CREAM
Zupa Grzybowa

½ lb. mushrooms
2 T butter
2 T flour
2 cups water

1 egg yolk
¼ cup sweet cream
1 cup milk
Salt and pepper

Wash and chop mushrooms. Cook in the butter under cover for 10 minutes. Stir in the flour and cook slowly until the mixture bubbles. Add water and simmer 15 minutes. Beat egg yolk with cream until well blended and add milk. Pour egg mixture slowly into mushrooms. Reheat to just below the boiling point, stirring constantly. Season to taste.

CLEAR MUSHROOM SOUP
Zupa Grzybowa Klarowna

2 qts. vegetable stock
6 large dry mushrooms or

1 cup chopped fresh mush-
    rooms
Chopped dill or parsley

Simmer mushrooms in vegetable stock for 1 hour. Strain. Chop parsley or dill fine and add to soup before serving. You may prefer not to strain the soup if you have used the fresh chopped mushrooms. Serve with **uszka** (page 31).

BARSHCH
Barszcz

2 qts. vegetable stock
    (page 24)
1 pt. beet **kwas** (page 19)

1 cup sour cream
2 T flour

Mix vegetable stock with beet **kwas.** Bring to boiling point and add flour blended with sour cream. Bring to boiling point again and serve with strips of cooked beets, fried croutons or boiled potatoes.

FISH SOUP
Zupa z Ryby

2 qts. vegetable stock
1 bay leaf
2 peppercorns

½ cup sweet cream
Fish or fish head
Chopped parsley

If you can spare 3 or 4 sunfish or a small pike, cook it with the vegetable stock and spices for 20 minutes. Lift fish out of soup carefully; strain soup and serve with boiled potatoes. If you have a large pike that you prefer to fry or broil, clean the head thoroughly and cook with vegetable stock and spices. Add half cup of sweet cream to soup just before serving.

YELLOW SPLIT PEA SOUP
Postna Grochówka

1 lb. yellow split peas
3 qts. water
¼ t pepper
2 t salt

3 bay leaves
4 whole allspice
4 whole peppercorns
1 cup diced carrots

Boil all ingredients except carrots slowly for about 4 hours or until peas are tender. Add carrots 2 hours before soup is done.

POTATO SOUP
Zupa Kartoflana

3 medium potatoes, sliced
2 stalks celery
1 large onion, sliced thin
2 carrots
1 sprig parsley

2 qts. water
3 T butter
1 T flour
1 cup top milk
Salt to taste

Cover vegetables with water, add seasoning and cook until well done. Force through sieve. Heat butter until light brown, stir in flour and let mixture cook until it bubbles and is well blended. Gradually add hot milk to the flour mixture and let simmer just below boiling point until mixture is smooth and thick. Add to strained vegetables and let simmer until smooth and thickened. Sprinkle with chopped parsley and serve with Egg Barley (page 30).

SAUERKRAUT SOUP
Kapuśniak

½ qt. sauerkraut
1 cup mushrooms, chopped
2 qts. water
Salt and pepper to taste

2 T butter
1 small onion
1 T flour

Rinse sauerkraut twice. Wash mushrooms. Cover sauerkraut and mushrooms with water and cook until tender (about 1½ hours). Chop onion and fry in butter and add to soup. Brown flour in the other tablespoon of butter until nut brown. Pour 3 tablespoons of soup into the browned flour, mix and add to soup. Bring to boiling point and serve.

25

BEER SOUP
Polewka z Piwa

1 qt. beer
4 egg yolks

4 t sugar
Croutons or cheese

Bring beer to boiling point. Beat egg yolks with sugar until lemon colored. Slowly mix half cup of the hot beer with yolks and then carefully add yolks to boiling beer, stirring constantly. Do not boil because the yolks will curdle. Serve with hot croutons or your favorite cheese.

WINE SOUP
Polewka z Wina

1 qt. red or white wine
2 cups water
1 stick cinnamon

4 whole cloves
5 egg yolks
5 t sugar

Bring the wine, water and spices to a boil. Strain. Beat the egg yolks with sugar until lemon-colored and slowly add the hot wine mixture, beating constantly until a thick foam forms at the top. Do be careful not to curdle the yolks. Serve in cups with wafers.

If you use the red wine, do not use egg yolks. Cover ½ cup sago with 2 quarts of boiling water and cook for 20 minutes, stirring well. When it is tender, add grated lemon rind, 4 whole cloves, ¼ teaspoon cinnamon to the wine and boil for a moment. Strain and add to the sago. Serve in a tureen, passing sugar, cinnamon and grated lemon rind in a sauce boat.

COLD SOUPS
ZUPY ZIMNE

CUCUMBER SOUP
Chłodnik

2 qts. sour cream
1 T green dill, cut fine
1 T green onion, cut fine
½ cup cooked beets and

young tops, chopped fine
1 t parsley, chopped very fine
1¼ cups chopped cucumbers
Salt and pepper

Peel and chop cucumbers, scald and set in refrigerator for a couple of hours. Combine all ingredients. Make this soup the day before. Serve very cold with 3 ice cubes in each plate. Serve with croutons or toasted Rye Krisp.

CUCUMBER SOUP
Chłodnik

1 qt. sour cream
1 qt. sour milk
1 cup diced cucumbers
1 cup cooked beets and young
   tops, chopped fine

1 T green dill, cut fine
1 T green onion, cut fine
6 hard-cooked eggs

Peel and dice cucumbers. Scald, rinse in cold water and set in refrigerator for 3 hours. Combine all ingredients. Serve very cold with quartered hard-cooked eggs, or hot boiled potatoes sprinkled with chopped crisp bacon.

APPLE SOUP
Chłodnik z Jabłek

5 or 6 medium tart apples
Sugar to taste

Sweet cream

Make a thin apple sauce, sweeten to taste and when cool, add enough sweet cream for soup consistency. Serve cold in cups.

BLUEBERRY SOUP
Zupa z Czernic

2 cups water
1 pt. blueberries
1/2 cup sugar

1 lemon thinly sliced
1/2 cinnamon stick
1/2 pt. heavy sour cream

Place water in sauce pan, add blueberries, sugar, lemon slices and cinnamon stick. Boil slowly for about 15 minutes, then strain. Let cool. After it is thoroughly chilled, stir in sour cream, mix thoroughly and serve. Serves 6.

"NOTHING" BUT DELICIOUS
Zupa Nic

1 qt. milk
6 eggs
1/2 cup sugar

2 t sugar
1/2 t vanilla
Dash of cinnamon or nutmeg

Separate the eggs. Beat yolks with 1/2 cup sugar until lemon colored. Beat whites until stiff and add 2 teaspoons sugar. Scald milk. With spoon place egg whites on the boiling milk and cook five minutes until firm. Lift meringues out carefully. Add 1/4 cup cold milk to yolks and slowly add to hot milk, stirring constantly. Return to fire for the mixture to thicken but do not bring to boiling point or the yolks will curdle. Cool slightly and add flavoring. Serve in bowls topped with meringues and dash of cinnamon or nutmeg. Delicious and excellent soup for children and convalescents.

ADDITIONS TO SOUPS
DODATKI DO ZUP

RICE
Ryż

½ cup rice   2 qts. salted boiling water

Wash rice in cold water. Add it slowly to the rapidly boiling water. Stir once to prevent sticking and cook for 20 minutes. Drain through colander and run hot water to wash off extra starch. Then cover colander with cloth and set over deep pan of boiling water to steam and dry out or "fluff."

RICE NOODLES
Kluski z Ryżu

2 cups cooked rice   1 T butter   2 eggs

Add butter and eggs to rice and mix very thoroughly. Drop from spoon into boiling soup.

EGG NOODLES
Makaron

1 large egg   1 cup flour
¼ t salt   ½ egg shell of water

Mound flour on a board. Make hole in center, drop in egg and salt. Mix with knife and add water. Knead until dough is smooth. Flour the board and roll out very thin. Place sheet of dough on a cloth and let dry until not the least sticky and yet not too brittle to handle. Sprinkle the sheet well with flour, fold into a tight roll. Slice the roll in thin threads, toss the threads up lightly on board to dry. Boil in salted water until the noodles rise to the top. Strain and give them a cold water bath. This is a small recipe but egg noodles may be made in quantity and stored in a covered jar.

~~~~~~

Bez pracy nie ma kołaczy.
Without work there is no bread.

For a larger quantity take:

5 eggs	4 cups flour
2 t salt	2 egg shells of water

Be sure to dry the noodles thoroughly before storing them in a jar.

Of course you can buy store noodles if you do not want to bother with homemade, but do make them. They are delicious and so easy to make.

EGG DROPS
Kluski Lane

2 eggs, beaten	1 T water
¼ t salt	½ cup flour

Mix ingredients and stir until smooth. Pour slowly from end of spoon into boiling soup, and let boil 2 to 3 minutes. If poured into soup from a considerable height, shape of drops will be improved.

CHIFFON NOODLES
Kluski z Piany

2 eggs	¼ t salt
2 T flour	

Separate the eggs. Beat whites and salt until stiff but not dry. Add yolks and beat slowly until mixed. Carefully fold in the flour and pour the mixture on boiling soup. Cover tightly and boil for 2 minutes. Uncover and turn. Break with spoon and serve in chicken soup with a slice of carrot and thin sprinkling of chopped parsley for garnish.

FRENCH NOODLES
Kluski Francuskie

1 T butter	4 eggs	2 T flour

Cream butter to a fluff. Separate eggs. Add yolks to butter one at a time, beating constantly. Beat egg whites until stiff but not dry. Add to butter and yolks. Lightly fold in the flour. Pour into boiling soup and cover. This will form a solid mass on top of soup. After 2 minutes, turn and cover, and they are ready. To serve, break noodles with spoon.

BEATEN NOODLES
Kluski Rozcierane

1 T butter	1 whole egg
2 egg yolks	1 heaping T flour

Cream butter to a fluff. Add yolks and continue beating until thick. Then add whole egg and beat again. Add flour lightly and mix well. Cook in boiling soup like French noodles.

29

EGG BALLS
Kluski z Żółtek

3 hard-cooked egg yolks   Salt and pepper
3 raw egg yolks   Pinch of nutmeg

Mash the cold cooked eggs to a powder. Add raw yolks and season. Mix to thick paste. Drop into boiling soup and serve immediately.

EGG BARLEY
Zacierki

1 egg   Flour
¼ t salt

Beat egg slightly with salt, add enough flour so that mixture can be kneaded into a **stiff ball.** Rub well with the hollow of the hand until small grains are formed or grate on coarse grater. Toss out lightly on a board to dry. Store in a covered jar. When ready to use, drop gradually into boliing soup or milk and let boil 5 to 10 minutes.

NOODLE PEAS
Groszek z Ciasta

½ cup milk   Salt
1 egg   Powdered sugar
1½ T flour

Gradually add milk to flour and stir to a smooth paste. Add egg and salt and beat well. Pour batter through coarse sieve into hot butter or friture (page 42). When it browns, lift out carefully. Sprinkle with powdered sugar and serve with fruit soups.

CUSTARD NOODLES
Kremik

2 cups cold meat stock   10 egg yolks

Beat yolks only until they are well blended. Add soup and mix well. Pour custard into small moulds and cook in steamer under cover until set. Serve one or two custards on each plate of soup.

CROQUETTES FOR SOUP OR BARSZCZ
Krokiety do rosołu lub barszczu

1 cup cooked mashed potatoes   2 eggs
1 cup cooked mashed   2 T bread crumbs
  vegetables   Salt and pepper
1 small onion, sauted in butter

Mix all ingredients. Form into 3 inch rolls, the width of a finger. Dip in bread crumbs and fry in butter. Pass with soup.

30

USHKA
Uszka

1 egg
½ cup water
2 T mashed potatoes,
(optional)

½ t salt
2 cups flour

Mound flour on kneading board. Beat egg with water and salt slightly and carefully pour into mound of flour. Mix and add the mashed potatoes. Knead until dough becomes elastic. Cover closely with warm bowl and let stand about 10 minutes. For easier handling, divide the dough in half. Roll out very thin, cut in 2 inch squares. Place half teaspoon of filling a little to one side on each square. Moisten edge with water. Fold over and press edges together. Join the two upper corners. Drop into salted boiling water and cook until they float to top.

Meat Filling for Ushka

1 small onion
3 T butter
Chopped cooked beef

Chopped mushrooms, cooked
(optional)
Salt and pepper

Run cooked beef through grinder. Chop onion fine and lightly brown in butter. Add chopped mushrooms and fry very slowly. Add meat and seasoning. Cool before using.

Meatless Filling

2 cups cooked chopped
mushrooms
1 T chopped onion
3 T butter
Salt and pepper
Fry onion in butter until light brown. Add chopped mushrooms and fry very slowly for 10 minutes. Add pepper and salt. Cool.

MEAT DUMPLINGS
Pulpety z Mięsa

½ lb. ground beef, veal
or pork
Small piece kidney fat,
ground fine
1 hard roll

2 eggs
Flour
Salt and pepper
1 t minced parsley

Mix all ingredients thoroughly. Put a little flour in the palm of your hand and roll small balls the size of a walnut. Cook in meat stock. Delicious with **barczcz.**

KNELKI

½ lb. cooked veal or breast   Salt
    of chicken   ½ cup sweet cream
1 slice dry bread

Chop meat fine and chop in mortar to a mass. Add moistened bread and salt. Mix well. Add cream by tablespoons. Continue to beat until the mass is light and fluffy. Drop in 2 inch lengths from side of spoon into boiling water. Cook until they float to top. Lift out carefully and serve with your choicest soups, or use as garnish with buttered crumbs.

MARROW DUMPLINGS
Pulpety

½ lb. marrow or   2 t. parsley, chopped fine
White beef suet from kidney   Salt and pepper to taste
1 cup bread crumbs   2 eggs

Remove membrane from marrow or suet. Chop fine. Add the eggs, salt, pepper, bread crumbs and parsley. Mix thoroughly but lightly. Form into small round balls, roll in flour and drop into slowly boiling soup for 10 minutes.

RAW POTATO DUMPLINGS
Kartoflane Kluski

2 cups raw potatoes   1½ cups flour
1 t salt   ½ cup bread crumbs
2 eggs

Grate potatoes fine and drain off brown liquid. Add the beaten eggs, salt, crumbs and flour to make a stiff dough. Drop into boiling salted water from wet spoon. Dumplings should be about 1½ inches long and ½ inch in diameter when cooked. They are done as soon as they float to top.

POTATO DUMPLINGS
Kartoflane Kluski

3 cups hot mashed potatoes   ½ cup flour
½ cup dry bread crumbs   Pinch of marjoram
2 egg yolks   2 egg whites
Salt and pepper to taste

Mix ingredients in the order given. Beat egg whites until stiff and fold in. Place on floured board and roll to pencil thickness. Cut into 2 or 3 inch strips, drop into salted boiling water. Boil until dumplings float to top. Drain and serve in soup. May be served on platter covered with chopped crisp bacon.

CROUTONS
Grzanki - Krutony

4 slices bread, 2 days old   Butter

Remove crusts from bread and cut into tiny cubes. Brown in oven and saute in butter. For cheese croutons, sprinkle with Parmesan cheese. With pea soup and potato soup serve rye bread croutons.

CROUTONS FOR FRUIT SOUPS
Grzanki do Zup Owocowych

Finger rolls, 2 days old   Butter
½ cup sweet cream   Powdered sugar

Slice finger rolls. Dip in cream and quickly saute in butter. Sprinkle with sugar. Without sugar, use as garnish for vegetables and poultry.

GRITS
Kasza

1 cup buckwheat grits   2 T butter
1 egg, slightly beaten   1 t salt
2 cups boiling water

Mix the grits and egg together thoroughly and cook over medium flame, stirring constantly until the kernels are separated and the mixture hard and dry. Add boiling water, butter and salt. Cover tightly and cook over low heat about 20 minutes. The grits must be dry when done, not damp.

~~~~~~

GOŚĆ W DOM, BÓG W DOM

"A guest in my home is God in my home"
This is our time honored greeting,
Our heritage from days of old
When Brotherhood was more than gold;
The host shared bread and salt with all:
The peasant, knight; the great and small,
And friends were made while eating.
—Victoria Janda

EASTER TRADITIONS

Spring comes to Poland early. The larks and the storks return on St. Joseph's day and in some years, earlier. The sun rises higher and higher into the sky. The ice breaks in the waters, the frost leaves the ground, and the grass pushes its tiny green blades into the warming air, afraid that snow may yet come. The buds on the trees swell; the black earth, beloved by the Pole, teeming with life after its winter rest, invites early sowing and planting. The cattle know that spring has come. All of nature responds and awakens; every spring brings a resurrection for her. Only man must wait for his resurrection. Yet each spring nature fills man with faith and courage to hope in the morrow.

Because the Pole lives very close to the soil, he too longs for a way to express the joy he feels in this glorious and sunny springtime. Here the church in its calendar year brings to him the Easter holy days. He prepares for them with six weeks of sincere fast and forbearance of simple pleasures. It is a long period of penitence and atonement during the last weeks of a cold and often dull, foggy winter. Then comes the Resurrection, the feast of triumph and of the termination of Lent and suffering. To the Pole the Holy Day never loses its meaning that all humanity was redeemed through the suffering and death of the Saviour.

Small wonder that with Easter dawn, after the spiritual feasts in the many churches, the Pole's table assumes such a prominent role in the day's festivity. All food which he eats that day is blessed by the priest. His breakfast is called Święcone. Then the egg, the symbol of life, is broken and shared with an exchange of good wishes. The Pole has no special menu for that day. There are no courses. Food aplenty is arranged upon a

34

large table. Meats in the form of long sausages, hams, loaves, cold roasts and suckling pig predominate. Deep dishes full of hard-cooked and decorated eggs, sauces, pastries—**babki, dziady, mazurki**—and a great variety of sweets complete the menu. In the center stands a lamb moulded of butter or pastry, holding the Polish flag. The table is decorated with sprigs of green leaves. Unlike Christmas, which is a day of family gatherings, Easter is an occasion of traditional Polish hospitality when everybody is invited and welcome. "Christ is risen—Allelujah!"

To this day, everywhere in the Polish communities on Saturday afternoon before Easter, baskets of food are brought to the churches and blessed by the priest.

MEATS
MIĘSA
BEEF

.Beef varies in quality. To safeguard you against paying for quality in meat which you do not get, the Government has made compulsory the grading of all meats with the exception of pork. Identify the grades on the meat with the letters "AA" for choice, "A" for good, "B" for commercial and "C" for utility. Low grades are inferior in tenderness and eating qualities. "AA" beef has a fresh bright red color, the fat is firm and white.

BEEF WITH HORSERADISH SAUCE
Sztuka Mięsa z Chrzanem

3 to 4 lbs. beef rump or
3 to 4 lbs. short ribs of beef

Meat from which the basic meat stock, **rosół,** was cooked, is often served with a garnish of **vegetables** or a favorite sauce. Less choice cuts of meat are chopped fine or ground and used as filling for **pierogi, naleśniki, uszka,** etc.

Horseradish Sauce

½ cup grated horseradish
1 cup sour cream
1 T flour
1 T butter

1½ t salt
2 T lemon juice or vinegar
1 t sugar

Melt butter in double boiler. Add horseradish, sour cream and flour and stir well to avoid lumps. Bring to boiling point and cook until thick. Add vinegar or lemon juice, salt and sugar. Serve hot or cold.

BRAISED BEEF
Najlepsza Sztuka Mięsa Biała

3 to 4 lbs. beef, cooked in soup
3 T butter
1 onion, sliced
1 bay leaf

4 peppercorns
Celery tops and parsley
½ cup soup stock
Salt to taste

Slightly brown the beef in melted butter. Add other ingredients and simmer over low heat until the liquid is absorbed. Keep meat tightly covered. Turn several times during cooking.

36

POT ROAST OF BEEF
Sztufada

4 lbs. beef
¼ lb. salt pork
3 T butter
1 jigger white wine or
    whiskey

Salt and pepper
4 whole carrots
1 sliced onion
2 bay leaves
4 peppercorns

Cut salt pork into small pieces. Make incisions in meat and stuff with salt pork. Brown meat in melted butter. Add other ingredients, cover tightly and simmer very slowly for 4 hours. Make gravy from meat sauce and serve with meat.

BEEF ROAST
Pieczeń Wołowa

4 to 5 lbs. beef rump
½ cup vinegar
½ t mixed whole spices
2 small onions
Salt and pepper

¼ lb. salt pork
2 cups water
1 cup sour cream
2 T flour

Cut salt pork into small pieces. Make incisions in the roast and fill with salt pork in two and three inch spaces. Place in earthenware vessel, cover with vinegar, water, spices, salt and onions. Let stand overnight.

The next day put meat and liquid into a roaster and bake uncovered at 325° until meat is tender, basting the meat at frequent intervals. Strain sauce in roaster and add the flour blended with sour cream. Stir well and boil for 3 minutes. Slice the beef, arrange on platter and cover with gravy.

HUSSAR ROAST
Pieczeń Huzarska

3 lbs. beef round
½ cup vinegar
¼ cup butter
½ cup meat stock
1 large onion, quartered

Stuffing:
2 t bread crumbs
½ t melted butter
2 medium onions, grated
1 egg
1½ t salt
¼ t pepper
1 T flour

Pound meat well and scald with hot vinegar. Dredge with flour, fry in butter and add stock and onion. Cover and simmer for 2 hours. Half hour before serving, take meat from pan, cut crosswise into thin slices, leaving every other slice not completely cut through. Combine bread crumbs, butter, egg and onion and place between the partially cut slices. Skewer meat with toothpicks. Return to pan, sprinkle with flour and cook for half hour. If necessary, add a little stock for the last cooking.

37

BEEF ROLL-UPS
Zraziki po Krakowsku

2 lbs. round steak	8 T butter, melted
1 cup bread crumbs	1 T chopped parsley
1 onion, grated	2 cups water
1 egg, beaten	Salt and pepper

Cut steak into thin pieces, about 4½ by 2 inches. Score, sprinkle with salt and pepper. Combine bread crumbs, egg, onion, 4 tablespoons melted butter, salt and pepper. Spread the dressing on each piece of meat, roll up and fasten with skewer or toothpick. Roll in flour and brown in remaining butter. Add 2 cups of water (meat stock, if you have it) and simmer 1½ hours. Remove toothpicks. Pour gravy over meat. Garnish with chopped parsley and mashed potatoes.

BROILED STEAK WITH MADEIRA AND MUSHROOMS
Polędwica z Maderą i Truflami

Porterhouse, T-Bone, or	Salt and pepper
Sirloin Steak	½ cup Madeira wine
Olive oil	2 ozs. button mushrooms
2 onions, sliced	1 bouillon cube

One hour before broiling, wipe steak with damp cloth and trim off surplus fat. Rub with olive oil and cover with sliced onions. Steak should be at room temperature when it goes under the broiler. When done, arrange steak on hot platter, sprinkle with salt and pepper and spread with butter. Bring wine and bouillon to boiling point. Add mushrooms and serve with steak. The onions may be sauteed and served.

RADECKI ROAST
Pieczeń Radeckiego

2 lbs. round steak	2 T butter
3 T butter	1 T bread crumbs
1 cup water	1 t sugar
1 lemon, peeled	2 egg yolks
3 T horseradish	Salt and pepper

Brown the meat in butter. Add water and simmer. When tender, remove from kettle. Make opening in meat. Slice lemon very thin and place in opening. Mix remaining ingredients and cover lemon slices. Roll and tie with thread. Return to kettle and cook slowly for 30 minutes. Sift flour over meat and pour 2 tablespoons of cream into sauce. Cook until flour, cream and sauce are well blended.

38

MEAT LOAF
Pieczeń Siekana - Klops

3 lbs. ground beef
1 lb. ground pork
¼ lb. kidney fat, chopped fine
1 cup bread crumbs, day old
1 onion, chopped fine
2 egg yolks
¼ lb. salt pork, chopped
3 T butter
1 T flour
½ t savory
½ cup cream
Salt and pepper

Fry onion in butter until transparent, not yellow. Combine the meat, kidney fat, salt pork, bread crumbs, onion, egg yolks and seasoning and mix very thoroughly with your hand. Shape into loaf, rub with butter and bake at 350° for one hour. Baste often. In the last 15 minutes, sprinkle flour on meat and add cream.

MEAT LOAF FILLED WITH BUCKWHEAT GRITS
Klops Nadziewany Kaszą

Meat loaf, prepared as above.
1 cup buckwheat grits
2 cups water
¼ lb. crisp chopped bacon

Salt
3 T butter
2 T flour

Wash grits and cook in double boiler with water, salt and bacon until tender. Carefully roll the meat on board to one inch thickness and fill center with grits. Roll into loaf, dredge with flour and brown quickly in butter. Bake 30 minutes in 400° oven.

BEEF BITKI IN CREAM
Bitki Wołowe w Śmietanie

2 lbs. ground beef
2 hard rolls soaked in milk
1 onion, chopped
2 egg yolks
2 egg whites, beaten

Salt and pepper
Flour
Pint of sour cream
Butter
1 cup chopped mushrooms

Saute onion in butter until transparent. Combine the meat, onion, yolks, rolls and seasoning. Mix well. Add beaten egg whites. Form in balls, roll in flour and brown slowly in butter. Add the sour cream and mushrooms. Cover and simmer for 30 minutes.

BEEF TONGUE
Ozór na Szaro

4 or 5 lb. beef tongue
3 qts. water
1 onion

2 bay leaves
5 peppercorns
Salt to taste

Boil tongue with other ingredients until tender, about 2 hours. Cool. Remove outside skin and roots. Slice thin. Save broth.

Sauce:
3 t sugar
3 t water
1 T butter
1 T flour
2 cups broth in which tongue was boiled

Small glass of wine
1 t vinegar or
2 t lemon juice
½ t lemon rind
½ cup raisins
½ cup chopped blanched almonds

Carmelize the sugar and water. Add butter, flour and broth and boil to the bubbling stage. Add remaining ingredients. Add sliced tongue and bring to a boil.

TRIPE
Flaczki

5 lbs. tripe
1 soup bone
1 onion, chopped
1 stalk celery
1 sprig parsley
1 sliced carrot

1 T flour
1 T butter
½ t marjoram
1 t ground ginger
Salt and pepper

Most meat markets now sell tripe already cooked, but if you cannot buy the cooked tripe, be sure you buy tripe that is cleaned and white. Cover the scraped and cleaned tripe with cold water and bring to boiling point. Pour off this water and cover the tripe with fresh water. Cook until tender, 3 to 4 hours. Let stand in this water until the next day. Pour off water. If you buy the cooked tripe, you will be saved all this work.

Cook the soup bone in about 2 quarts of cold water with the onion, celery, parsley and carrot for 1 hour. Cut the cooked tripe into strips about 3 inches long, ½ inch wide. Add to the soup bone and vegetables. Cook together for about 4 hours or until tripe is tender. Brown flour in butter in frying pan, add a little soup stock to make a thin paste, add to tripe. Add spices and cook for five more minutes. Serve with Marrow Dumplings (page 32).

Tripe is served as a soup or meat course.

40

CABBAGE ROLLS
Gołąbki

1 lb. ground beef	1 onion, chopped fine
1/2 lb. ground pork or veal	2 T butter
1/2 cup rice	Salt and pepper
1 egg	

Remove core from whole head of cabbage with sharp knife. Scald the cabbage in boiling water. Remove a few leaves at a time as they wilt. Cool before using.

Wash rice in cold water and stir into 2 quarts of rapidly boiling salted water. Boil 10 minutes and strain. Run cold water through rice in strainer. This rice is only half cooked now.

Saute onion in butter only until it becomes transparent. Do not let it turn yellow. Combine with meat, egg, rice and seasonings and mix well. Spread each leaf with meat, about half inch thick, fold the two opposite sides and roll, starting with one of the open ends. Fasten with toothpick.

To cook—place cabbage rolls in baking dish, cover with 5 slices of bacon and roast uncovered for 2 hours at 300°. Baste from time to time. Or brown the Gołąbki in frying pan, add 1 cup water or tomato puree and simmer slowly for 2 hours. Watch closely and add more water if necessary. Gołąbki may be served with mushroom sauce, tomato sauce or sour cream. When reheated the next day, they are even more delicious.

KOLDUNY
Kołduny

1/2 lb. tenderloin of beef	1 t marjoram
1/2 lb. lamb	Meat stock
1/4 lb. kidney fat	Buttered bread crumbs
2 onions, grated	Salt and pepper
2 T butter	

Remove all sinew from meat and suet. With sharp knife cut meat into small slivers. Chop kidney fat to a fine mass. Barely heat the grated onion in butter for flavor. Add seasoning and mix all ingredients well.

Prepare dough as for **uszka** (page 31). Roll out very thin and cut small rounds. Place a small amount of the filling to one side on the round. Bring the edges together and seal tight. Be frugal with the filling because the suet and meat will swell in the cooking and need space. Boil **kołduny** in meat stock for 10 minutes. Serve immediately in soup plates with half cup of soup. Cover with buttered crumbs. Serve as soup course. They must be small because they are never cut at the table.

41

FRITURE
Frytura

Beef kidney fat   Water

Friture is a clear fat made from the suet which encloses the beef kidney. It is excellent for all deep fat frying. It imparts no odor to foods and does not have the high burning point of butter. After use, it may be strained and used many times. It does not saturate the food it fries. It is important to keep this distinction in mind—it is to be used for deep fat frying only, never for sauteing. It is as digestible as butter.

Ask your butcher for the suet from the beef kidney. Remove all membrane, cut into pieces or run through the coarse blade of the grinder. Soak in ice water for 24 hours. To cook, cover with cold water and simmer until water cooks out. Strain into earthenware vessel and keep in cool place. Use for frying fish, potatoes, pastries, fritters, pączki, chruścik and many other good foods.

VEAL

Veal is the flesh of calves. Choice veal is of a pinkish gray color and its fat is white. While veal is young meat and should be tender, it requires longer cooking than beef. There is much connective tissue in veal that requires long, slow cooking to soften it. Veal is always cooked well-done.

BREADED VEAL CHOPS
Kotlety Cielęce Bite

Loin or rib veal chops   2 T cold water
Salt and pepper   1 egg
Flour   Bread crumbs
1 cup cream

Pound veal chops, salt, pepper and dredge with flour. Add water to egg and mix lightly with fork. Dip chops in egg, then in crumbs, and fry. Be sure to use part butter in frying the chops for no other meat absorbs the flavor of butter as veal does because it is a lean meat. When chops are nicely browned on both sides, add cream and set into oven for 30 minutes at 350°.

VEAL CUTLETS
Kotlety Cielęce

2 lbs. veal steak   5' t cream
½ cup butter   1 t flour
1 T chopped parsley   5 truffles
Salt and pepper

Chop veal, not too fine. Melt butter. Add parsley and other ingredients. Last, the meat and mix well together. Form the

42

cutlets in the palm of your hand. Each cutlet should be about 3 inches long. Cook 5 or 6 minutes as you would beefsteak. Put little paper handles on ends of cutlets. Serve with creamed mushrooms.

VEAL CHOPS
Sznycle Cielęce

5 veal chops
3 T butter
6 T sherry
¼ cup sliced mushrooms
2 onions, chopped fine

3 T flour
2 cups chicken stock
3 bay leaves
Salt and pepper

Remove meat from bone and cut each chop into two thin slices. Pound thin. Brown in butter and add sherry. Remove meat and put into skillet the mushrooms, onions, flour and chicken stock. Bring to boiling point and return veal. Add bay leaves, salt and pepper. Cook at a slow simmer for 30 minutes. Arrange veal on platter and cover with sauce.

VEAL ROLLS
Zraziki Cielęce

4 lbs. boned rolled veal leg
2 T butter
Salt and pepper
Flour for dredging

1 onion
4 whole cloves
Parsley

Sprinkle meat with salt and pepper, dredge with flour. When fat is hissing hot, lay meat in and brown, turning frequently. A 4 pound piece will take 20 minutes to brown. Add a little water or meat stock, just enough to keep meat from burning. Cover closely and roast slowly for 3 hours.

When meat is braised, cut in thin slices. Make a puree of mushrooms lightly mixed with Bechamel sauce (page 77) and spread between each slice. Hold all together with a string, leaving one long end to pull off when meat is on platter. Replace the meat in roaster, cover top with Bechamel Sauce mixed with Parmesan cheese. Sprinkle again with Parmesan cheese and brown in oven.

Serve with large mushrooms stuffed with own meat chopped up with sauce and cooking juice from pan. Serve with peas and small round fried potatoes.

VEAL WITH PAPRIKA
Paprykarz Cielęcy

3 lbs. veal breast or shoulder
3 T butter
1 onion, sliced
2 cups sour cream

1 T flour
1 T paprika
1 cup hot water
Salt and pepper

All veal for stewing should be blanched. That is, it should be placed in hot water, brought to a boil, and rinsed with cold water. Lightly brown onion in butter, add meat and cup of hot water and simmer gently for 2 hours. When meat is tender, add salt and pepper. Mix the flour with sour cream and add to meat. Heat thoroughly and serve generously sprinkled with paprika.

VEAL ROAST
Pieczeń Cielęca

4 or 5 lbs. veal rump or
   shoulder
1/4 lb. salt pork
Garlic
1/4 t allspice
Dash of mace
Dash of cloves
Salt and pepper
2 bay leaves

1/2 t thyme
1/2 t sage
1/4 cup flour
3 T butter
1 onion
2 celery stalks
1 parsnip
4 carrots
1 cup boiling water

Wipe meat with damp cloth. Make incisions in meat with sharp knife and fill with bits of garlic and diced salt pork. Sprinkle meat with the seven spices. Rub well with flour. Brown the bouquet vegetables in the butter. They should be diced fine. Brown veal in another pan and add to vegetables. Add the boiling water, cover tightly, and simmer about 3 hours.

STUFFED VEAL ROAST
Pieczeń Cielęca

Veal loin or veal leg
Stuffing:
2 T butter
2 onions, sliced
1/2 cup celery, minced
1/2 lb. pork tenderloin, minced

1/8 t paprika
1/2 t salt
1 t dill, minced
1 cup sour cream
2 cups soft bread crumbs

Saute onion in butter lightly, add celery and dill and cook 3 minutes. Add sour cream and minced pork browned in butter or drippings. Add seasoning and simmer 20 minutes. Mix with bread crumbs and allow to cool. Slice veal and spread stuffing between slices. Tie together and place in roaster. Serve with creamed mushrooms.

44

VEAL WITH KIDNEY
Cielęcina z Nerką

Veal loin with kidney and
  flank
Flour
Salt and pepper
Stuffing:
2 cups soft caraway rye
  bread crumbs

1 egg, slightly beaten
2 T melted butter
2 T chopped onion
2 T minced parsley
3 T cream
½ lb. flank, ground

Have the butcher cut the veal loin roast with kidney and flank attached. Have top of loin bone sawed the thickness of each chop, but not cut through. Remove fat from kidney. Mix stuffing and place on top and around kidney. Bring the flank over to cover the stuffing and tie securely with string. Dredge meat with flour and season. Roast covered 25 minutes per pound in 325° oven. Last half hour remove cover to brown the roast.

STUFFED VEAL BREAST
Mostek Cielęcy Nadziewany

4 lbs. breast of veal
1 t salt
4 T melted butter
½ t marjoram
Stuffing:
2 cups dry bread
1 t salt

¼ t pepper
½ cup milk
2 T melted butter
1 egg, beaten
1 t parsley, minced
1 small onion, chopped

Wash meat and wipe dry. Cut pocket in veal breast with sharp knife. Soak bread in milk for 10 minutes. Squeeze out excess milk. Brown onion in butter. Cool, add bread, seasoning and egg. Toss lightly. Fill pocket and fasten with skewer. Brush meat with melted butter, salt and sprinkle with marjoram. Roast uncovered for 3 hours at 325°. Cover during the last half hour.

LAMB

Lamb is the flesh of young sheep. All cuts of lamb are tender. It is served medium-done and well-done but never lukewarm because the fat cakes rapidly. The meat of lamb is dark red in color and the fat is a delicate white. Mutton is the flesh of mature sheep and requires longer cooking periods.

ROAST LEG OF LAMB
Pieczeń Barania z Pieca

1 leg of lamb	Garlic or garlic salt
Salt and pepper	Vinegar

To properly age lamb, saturate muslin cloth with vinegar and wrap meat. Then wrap in heavy brown paper and bury in your garden for five days. Never bury twice in the same place, however, for it will absorb a musty odor.

Remove excess fat and sinew. Rub with garlic salt or make incisions and fill with bits of garlic bud. Scald with hot vinegar, season and let stand for 2 hours. Roast at 325° for 30 to 35 minutes per pound until tender. Baste frequently. Leg of lamb is excellent when removed from oven when half done and braised in cream under cover until done.

LAMB ROAST WITH CREAM
Pieczeń Barania Duszona Ze Śmietaną

Rolled lamb shoulder	1 onion, sliced
1/2 cup butter	2 T vinegar
Celery tops	Flour
Parsley	1 cup cream
Small slice salt pork	1/4 cup chopped mushrooms
5 juniper berries	

Brown meat in butter. Add all but last three ingredients. Cook covered until tender, turning often. When nearly done, remove from kettle, dust meat with flour, strain juice. Return meat and juice and add cream. Continue cooking until done.

LAMB WITH RICE
Potrawa z Baraniny z Ryżem

Lamb breast	1 cup rice
2 qts. water	1/2 cup chopped mushrooms
1 onion	2 egg yolks
Celery tops	1/2 cup buttered crumbs
Parsley	Salt and pepper
2 carrots	

Cook first 6 ingredients until meat is tender. Remove meat. Wash rice, add to meat stock. Bake in oven at 350° for 40 minutes. Add mushrooms and egg yolks and stir well. Place the cooked meat on top, cover with buttered crumbs and continue to bake for 20 minutes in 300° oven.

46

PORK

Choice pork is pink in color interlarded with pure white fat. All cuts of pork are tender. Pork is juicier when it is cooked slowly for a long time than if cooked rapidly. Rapid cooking drives off the fat that contains much of the flavor of pork. Pork should always be cooked to the well-done stage.

ROAST LOIN OF PORK
Schab Pieczony

4 to 5 lbs. pork loin	1 t ground mustard
1½ T flour	½ t sage
1 t salt	¼ t black pepper
½ t sugar	

Mix the ingredients and rub thoroughly into the loin. Roast at 325° uncovered from 4 to 5 hours, until tender.

A good crusty topping is made as follows:

1½ cups apple sauce	¼ t cinnamon
½ cup brown sugar	¼ t ground cloves

After meat has baked one and one-half hours, spread it generously with the topping and continue roasting until tender.

SUCKLING PIG
Prosię Pieczone

1 suckling pig	Fat for brushing
1 apple	Salt and white pepper
1 potato	

Clean pig, wash well inside and out with clear water. Rub well with salt. Sprinkle with white pepper inside and out. Stuff the cavity with dressing and sew up with linen thread or white cord. Cover ears and tail with pieces of well-greased paper. Place in roaster, brush with a little fat and roast at 375° for 2½ hours, basting every 15 minutes. Pig's mouth should be opened and a potato inserted. After roasting, remove the potato and place an apple in the mouth. If you want the skin of the pig to be soft, baste with hot stock; if you want it to be crusty, baste with oil or melted butter. Remove pig to hot platter and garnish with parsley or watercress.

Dressing:	1 t salt
1 loaf dry white bread	1 t pepper
Pig's liver	2 T parsley, minced
2 eggs	1 onion
4 T butter	1 t celery salt

Soak bread in milk. Press out surplus moisture and flake with fork. Chop onion and saute in butter, add chopped liver. Combine all ingredients and toss lightly.

Maciek zebrał, Maciek zjadł
Maciek gathered, Maciek ate.

KEESH-KA
Kiszka

3 lbs. pork steak
2 lbs. coarse buckwheat grits

½ t rubbed marjoram
Salt and pepper

Chop meat into coarse bits. Cover with water and boil until tender. Add salt, pepper and marjoram. Wash the buckwheat grits, cover with the liquid from cooked meat, and steam in double boiler for half hour. Combine the two mixtures. If you have sausage casings, stuff the mixture into the casings. It will keep very well in a mold in the refrigerator. Heat before serving.

DARK KEESH-KA
Kiszka z Krwią

4 pig's feet, split
2 lbs. pig's snouts
1 lb. pork steak
1 onion
4 whole black peppers
1 T salt
3 lbs. pork liver

5 lbs. coarse buckwheat grits
6 large onions
1 T ground allspice
2 T ground marjoram
Salt and pepper
1 pt. fresh pig's blood

Cover with hot water the first six ingredients and cook until tender. Scald liver, save the liquid from liver and add it to the pork stock. Remove meat from bones and put through food grinder. Chop the 6 onions and put into hot stock. Wash buckwheat grits and add to liquid. Cook slowly for half hour. Add chopped meat and liver and rest of spices. Salt and pepper to taste. Continue to cook slowly until the grits are tender. If mixture becomes dry, add meat stock or water. When grits are tender, remove from fire and cool. Add blood and mix well. Stuff into casing, tie at intervals to make sausages and cook slowly in boiling water for 20 minutes. If you do not have casings, **kiszka** will keep well in loaf pans. Serve either hot or cold. To heat, slice and fry in butter or shortening until golden brown on both sides. Recipe makes about 12 pounds of sausage.

Wszystkie stare czasy są dobre.
All times are good when old.

48

POLISH SAUSAGE
Kiełbasa

1½ lbs. pork loin or butt
½ lb. veal
Salt and pepper

1 bud of garlic
1 t whole mustard seed
3 T water

Remove meat from bones, cut into small pieces and run through coarse knife of food grinder. Add 3 tablespoons water, pound the garlic, add the seasoning. Mix very thoroughly and stuff casing. The sausage is then ready for smoking. If you do not have facilities for smoking, place the sausage in baking dish, cover with cold water and bake in oven, 350°, until the water is absorbed.

CASSUBIAN HEADCHEESE
Panas Kaszubski

1 pig's head
2 large onions
6 whole allspice
Salt and pepper

2 bay leaves
2 lbs. dry white bread
½ t cinnamon

Remove eyes and teeth from pig's head. Have the head chopped in quarters. Wash thoroughly, cover with water, add onion, allspice, bay leaves, salt and pepper. Cook until tender. Remove meat from bones and chop into coarse pieces. Cut bread into cubes, mix with meat and meat stock. Return to fire, add cinnamon and simmer slowly for 20 minutes, stirring to prevent burning. Pour into mold or crock. After it is set and cold, remove fat from top. Slice and heat before serving.

JELLIED PIGS FEET
Galareta

4 pig's feet, cut in halves
2 pork shanks
1 onion, well browned
1 stalk celery, chopped
1 sprig parsley, cut fine
Salt

1 clove garlic
5 whole peppers
5 whole allspice
4 bay leaves
1 T vinegar

Wash feet and shanks. Put into large kettle and cover with water. Bring to boiling point and skim. Add onion, celery, parsley, garlic and spices and simmer covered, very slowly about 4 hours or until meat comes off bones easily. Cool, strain, remove the bones and spices. Return meat to liquid, add salt and vinegar and pour into loaf or tube pan. Set in refrigerator until firm. Scrape fat from top. Garnish with cooked carrot slices, lemon slices and hard-cooked eggs.

SMOKED HAM
Szynka

If you plan to boil your ham, be sure to get an unskinned ham. A ham with the skin removed will not be as tasty after boiling. Wash the ham well and soak for four hours in cold water. Place in cooking vessel, cover with cold water, add a dozen whole peppers, 6 bay leaves and boil until tender. Test by moving the small bone at tip of ham. If you can move it easily, ham is tender. Keep in this liquid until ready to serve, if it is to be served hot. Remove skin, slice and serve with horseradish and green peas.

If the ham is to be served cold, let it remain in the liquid until it becomes cold. Then lift out, remove the skin and slice.

A ham cooked in this way, is excellent when it is garnished and put in the oven to brown. Garnish the ham by scoring the top. Cover lightly with brown sugar and powdered mustard and decorate with 25 whole cloves. Keep in oven at 350° for about an hour depending on the size of ham.

Another way to prepare ham is to soak it overnight in cold water. Rub it with a mixture of brown sugar, mustard and powdered cloves. Envelop it in rye bread dough thick with caraway seeds. Bake in a slow oven. At the last moment before use, strip off the crusty cover, and sprinkle it again with sugar, mustard and cloves and pop it into the oven to brown. This will give you a very succulent ham.

Today most of the hams in the markets are ready cooked or tenderized. Our recipes are for raw unskinned smoked hams.

SAUERKRAUT WITH PORK
Kapusta z Wieprzowiną

4 pig's feet	4 whole peppers
3 lbs. neck bones	½ t celery seed
or 3 lbs. spare ribs	1 qt. sauerkraut
1 large onion	½ t caraway seed
1 bud garlic	½ minced apple
4 whole allspice	3 T barley
1 bay leaf	Salt and pepper

Split and chop meat. Brown in lard and add the onion quartered, garlic, allspice, bay leaf, whole peppers and celery seed. Season to taste. Cover meat with boiling water and cook until meat is half done. Remove a cup of the liquid for gravy. Add sauerkraut, caraway seed, apple and barley and cook until meat is tender. Serve raw potato dumplings with gravy.

50

SAUERKRAUT WITH PORK
Kapusta z Żeberkami

2 lbs. spare ribs
1 qt. sauerkraut
1 large onion, quartered

¼ t caraway seed
3 qts. cold water

Cover spare ribs with cold water and bring to boiling point. Skim, add onion, sauerkraut and caraway seed and simmer uncovered for two hours or until meat is tender. Add no salt. The brine in the sauerkraut is salty.

FRIED LIVER
Wątroba

1 lb. beef or pork liver
3 T butter
1 cup bread crumbs

2 onions
1 cup vinegar
Salt and pepper

Pour the boiling vinegar over the liver. Drain and cut in 2-inch pieces. Season and roll in bread crumbs. Fry sliced onion in butter, then fry liver in same butter. Arrange liver on fried onion and pour brown gravy around.

KIDNEY STEW
Nerki Duszone

3 beef kidneys
1 T chopped onion
3 T flour

3 T butter
2 cups water
Pepper and salt

Split the kidneys, remove core, skin and hard membrane. Soak in cold salted water for half hour. Drain and slice thin. Saute in butter and flour for 10 minutes until nicely browned. Add water, onion and seasonings, cover and simmer 20 minutes.

LIVER LOAF
Pasztet z Wątróbek

1 lb. liver (any kind)
1 onion
1 egg, well beaten
1 T chopped celery

¼ lb. bacon
1 cup bread crumbs
1 T chopped parsley
Salt and pepper

Cover liver with boiling water and let stand for 10 minutes, then drain and dry. Mince the liver, bacon and onion. Combine all ingredients and mix thoroughly. Pack into greased loaf pan and bake 1 hour in moderate oven. Excellent for sandwiches and hors d'oeuvres.

51

PASH-TET
Pasztet

1½ lbs. calf liver
½ lb. veal
½ lb. pork from neck
½ lb. lamb or duck
¼ lb. bacon
2 stalks celery
2 onions
2 carrots
2 sprigs parsley
1 parsnip

1 bay leaf
½ t. marjoram
10 juniper berries
6 dry mushrooms
4 slices dry bread
6 eggs
6 crisp bacon strips
1 jigger Madeira wine
Salt and pepper

Soak liver in milk over night. Cook meats, mushrooms, vegetables and spices for about 3 hours. In the last hour, add calf liver. Over-cooking toughens liver. Strain the mixture and run through fine blade of food grinder 4 times. Remove crusts from bread and moisten with meat stock. Add bread, wine and stock to meats. Add eggs, one at a time, beating hard after each addition. Season with salt and pepper to taste. Fry bacon strips crisp. Butter a mold, sprinkle with bread crumbs and arrange bacon strips in a pattern. Fill with mixture and bake for 30 minutes at 350°. Serve hot or cold. Excellent for appetizers or canapes. Delicious with Tartar Sauce if served hot.

52

POULTRY AND GAME
DRÓB I ZWIERZYNA

There is an abundance of poultry in Poland. It is always sold alive. An old cook book says "Never use old poultry, for no matter how you prepare it, you can make nothing good of it. Young poultry has full thick legs. That characteristic loses itself in time. An old chicken has thin legs and a thin neck, and the skin on the drum stick is slightly blue. A good turkey you will know by its white flesh and white fat; never buy one that has long hairs in the skin and the feathers on the drumsticks of a purple color. A good goose you will know by the fullness of its wing and the tenderness of the lower part of the beak which on bending should snap easily; its fat should be white and transparent.

Use broilers at any time of the year; hens when they stop laying eggs; capons in the winter; ducks and geese from October to the end of January; turkeys from October to the end of January. Never cook poultry on the day you kill it. In warm weather, kill turkeys two days before cooking; in the winter, kill them from two to five days before you need them. The same rule applies to ducks and geese. Broilers and pigeons may be used immediately, but they, too, become more tender if they are kept a day after killing.

ROAST TURKEY
Indyk Pieczony

1 hen turkey	1 sliced onion
Salt	2 stalks celery
¼ t ground ginger	Stuffing

Pull out the pinfeathers. Then singe off the hairs over a flame quickly so as not to darken or scorch the skin. Cut off the head and feet. Scrub the bird with a brush. Rinse thoroughly and wipe dry. Cut out the oil sac on top of the tail.

To draw the bird, first slit the skin lengthwise at the back of the neck. Slip the skin down and without tearing outer skin,

53

remove windpipe and crop. Cut the neck off short without the skin and save it together with the wing tips, gizzard and heart for making broth to use in the gravy.

When drawing turkeys, chickens, or capons, cut crosswise of the body through the skin under the tail, making the cut only large enough to put the hand in. Leave a band of skin and flesh under the tail so that the legs can be securely tucked in after the bird is stuffed. The legs of ducks and geese are too short to tuck in, so make the cut for drawing them lengthwise of the body.

Insert the hand through the cut into the body cavity and draw out the entrails, heart, liver and gizzard. Be careful to remove every part of the lungs, which are located on each side of the backbone and between the ribs. The kidneys are in a hollow near the end of the backbone; remove them, too. After the body cavity is absolutly clean, the bird should be washed with cold water and wiped dry inside and out.

When ready to roast, sprinkle the inside with salt and ground ginger. Fill the body cavity and neck with any of the following stuffings. Do not pack the stuffing—allow room for stuffing to expand. Fill the bird with hot stuffing, if it is to be cooked at once. It may be more convenient to stuff the bird the day before it is to be cooked; if so, put the stuffing in cold and keep the bird well chilled so there will be no danger of spoilage.

Tuck the legs under the band of skin. Put a stitch through the skin at end of breastbone and wrap the cord around the legs and under the tail to help hold the legs in place. Lightly stuff the loose skin at the base of the neck. Fold end of neck skin toward the back and fasten with stitches. Tie the wings across the back close to the body.

Rub the turkey all over with butter, sprinkle with salt. If the bird is very lean, lay several strips of salt pork or bacon over it. Add a sliced onion and 2 stalks of celery. Bake uncovered until tender, in 325° oven.

STUFFING
Nadzienie

Turkey liver, chopped fine	2 eggs
1 onion, minced	1 cup celery, cut fine
6 T butter	1/2 t thyme
8 cups stale bread	1/4 t mace
Broth to moisten	Salt and pepper

Fry onion in butter until it becomes transparent, not brown. Add chopped liver and celery and fry. Moisten bread slightly. Mix all the ingredients and stuff turkey. You may add almond halves or half cup of black raisins and teaspoon of sugar.

54

RICE STUFFING
Nadzienie z Ryżu

2 cups uncooked rice
2 t salt

1 cup chopped mushrooms
Other ingredients as above,
    substitute rice for bread

Wash rice in cold water. Cover with boiling water, add salt and cook for 20 minutes. Drain; wash with hot water; dry and fluff by shaking colander over steam for 10 minutes. Fry the mushrooms with the liver, onions and celery. Combine all ingredients and stuff turkey.

CHESTNUT STUFFING
Farsz z Kasztanów

2 qts. chestnuts
½ cup butter
½ cup minced onion
¼ cup chopped parsley

2 cups chopped celery
2 t salt
¼ t pepper
1 t poultry seasoning

Cook chestnuts in boiling water for 20 minutes, remove the shell and brown skin while hot, and grate. Melt the butter and cook the onion, parsley and celery. Add chestnuts and seasoning. Mix well and stuff the bird.

SMOTHERED TURKEY
Indyk z Sosem

Turkey, cut at joints
1 qt. hot water
1 T butter

6 Polish dry mushrooms
Salt and pepper

Put ingredients in sauce pan and simmer until turkey is tender. Then make the following sauce:

1 T butter
1 T flour
1 cup turkey stock
Salt to taste

¼ t grated lemon rind
Pinch of ground mace
3 egg yolks

Melt butter, add flour and blend. Add turkey stock and simmer until thick. Add lemon rind and mace. Strain and add egg yolks. Carefully heat to below boiling point to prevent curdling of egg yolks. Arrange turkey on platter. Cover with sauce. Garnish with chopped mushrooms, cauliflower and asparagus.

LEFT-OVER ROAST TURKEY
Potrawa z Indyka Pieczonego

Turkey bones
3 cups cold water
Salt to taste
½ t sugar

¼ t ginger
2 t lemon juice
Turkey meat

Cover bones with water, bring to boiling point. Add remaining ingredients with exception of meat, and simmer until the flavor of the bones has been extracted and liquid cooked down. Add turkey meat, heat thoroughly and serve with short breads.

TURKEY CUTLETS
Kotleciki z Indyka

White meat of turkey
3 egg yolks
1 T butter
Salt and pepper

Lemon juice
Mushroom sauce
Green peas

Separate the cooked white meat from bones. Chop very fine through food grinder. Add egg yolks, butter and seasoning. Form into cutlets. Place in buttered baking pan and roast in 375° oven for 15 minutes When they brown on one side, sprinkle with lemon juice and turn. Serve with mushroom sauce (page 78) and buttered green peas.

STUFFED ROAST CAPON
Kapłon z Farszem

1 capon   Salt

Sprinkle the inside of the capon with salt. Make stuffing as follows:

¼ lb. pork back fat
½ lb. veal
Liver of capon
3 egg yolks

10 sardines
2 cups bread crumbs
¼ t lemon rind, grated
3 egg whites, beaten stiff

Cook veal with pork fat until tender. Cook the liver. Remove bones from sardines. Chop the meats, liver and sardines to a fine mass. Add the bread crumbs, lemon rind, butter and egg yolks. Mix well and fold in beaten egg whites. Stuff capon and rub with salt and butter. Bake at 325° until tender. Baste often.

ROYAL CHICKEN
Kura po Królewsku

Spring chicken
½ cup butter
1 large onion
Salt and pepper

1 cup hot water
2 cups sour cream
1 t paprika

Cut chicken in pieces. Saute onion in butter and when it becomes transparent, add chicken and fry very carefully until brown. Salt and pepper to taste. Add hot water, cover and simmer chicken until tender. When nearly done, add sour cream and sprinkle with paprika. Heat through and serve.

56

FRIED CHICKEN
Kurczęta z Pieca

Broiling chickens
Salt and pepper
1 egg, slightly beaten
½ cup flour

1 cup bread crumbs
5 T butter
1 cup sweet cream
2 T water

Cut chickens at joints. Season with salt and pepper. Dredge with flour, dip in egg mixed with water, then in bread crumbs Brown in butter. Add the cream and roast covered for about 1 hour at 350°.

SMOTHERED STUFFED CHICKEN
Nadziewane Kurczątko Duszone

1 broiling chicken
Salt
½ cup butter
Stuffing:
Chicken liver, chopped

1 t dill, finely chopped
1 cup dry bread crumbs
2 T butter
Salt and pepper

To make stuffing, fry chopped liver in butter. Add dill and bread crumbs. Rub inside of chicken with salt. Stuff chicken. Place in earthenware casserole, sprinkle with salt and cover with butter. Cook under cover at 350° until tender.

ROAST STUFFED CHICKEN
Nadziewane Kurczątko Pieczone

1 broiling chicken
1 hard roll
Milk to moisten
4 T butter

1 whole egg, 1 yolk, beaten
2 T bread crumbs
1 T minced parsley
Salt and pepper

Clean, wash and wipe broiler dry. Rub inside with salt. Mix other ingredients for stuffing and stuff the chicken. Rub with salt and butter and bake in oven at 350° for 1 hour.

YOUNG CHICKEN POLISH STYLE
Potrawa z Kurcząt Po Polsku

1 broiler, quartered
2 cups water
1 stalk celery
1 carrot
1 sprig parsley
2 dry Polish mushrooms

Salt
1 T butter
1 T flour
½ cup wine
2 egg yolks

Cover broiler with water. Bring to boiling point, add vegetables, mushrooms and salt. Simmer for about 1 hour until tender. Heat butter, add flour and blend. Add remaining chicken soup stock and cook until thick. Add the chopped cooked mushrooms and wine. Slowly stir in the egg yolks and add chicken. Heat thoroughly but do not cook. Serve with mashed potatoes.

57

YOUNG CHICKEN IN DILL SAUCE
Kurczęta z Sosem Koperkowym

1 broiler, quartered	1 cup sweet cream
1 T butter	1 T flour
2 cups water	1 t lemon juice
Salt and pepper	1 t chopped green dill

Smother the chicken in butter and water until tender. Season to taste. When done, add the cream mixed with flour, the lemon juice and dill. Bring to a boil. Serve on a bed of rice or with cauliflower covered with buttered crumbs.

YOUNG CHICKEN WITH GOOSEBERRY SAUCE
Potrawa z Kurcząt z Agrestem

1 broiler, quartered	½ t sugar
1 T butter	½ cup under-ripe goose -
1 T flour	berries
1 cup chicken stock	

Cook chicken as above in recipe for Young Chicken Polish style. Heat butter, add flour and thin with chicken stock. When thickened, add sugar and the gooseberries. Bring to boiling point, add chicken. You may prefer the sauce strained.

YOUNG CHICKEN WITH VEGETABLES
Kurczęta z Jarzynkami

1 broiler, quartered	1 carrot
Salt	½ cup green peas
2 T butter	4 stalks asparagus
1 bouillon cube	4 cauliflower flowerets
1 t parsley, chopped	1 t dill, chopped

Blanch vegetables with hot water. Place vegetables in bottom of kettle, add butter. Cover with chicken. Salt to taste. Add the bouillon cube and simmer covered for 40 to 50 minutes, until chicken is tender.

CHICKEN CUTLETS
Kotlety z Kurcząt

Individual serving:	1 egg
½ breast young chicken	Salt and pepper to taste
1 t butter	Fine dried bread crumbs

Pound chicken breast very thin. Chill butter thoroughly. Add seasonings to butter and knead into rolls about half inch thick and 2 inches long. Chill these rolls in a bowl of cracked ice. In the center of each half chicken breast place roll of butter and fasten the two firmly together with toothpicks. It is important to fold the chicken so securely around the chilled butter that no butter can leak out when it melts. Roll in fine crumbs, dip in beaten egg diluted with a little water and roll again in crumbs. Fry in deep hot fat until golden brown. Drain and place in a hot oven for a few minutes.

58

CHICKEN IN YELLOW SAUCE
Potrawka z Kury

1 soup chicken	Parsley
3 qts. cold water	Carrot
1 onion	Salt
Celery tops	

Cut chicken at joints. Cover with water, add other ingredients, cover tightly and cook until tender. If soup boils down, do not add hot water until you have removed the chicken. Strain soup and serve with your favorite addition (page 28).

Yellow Sauce:	2 cups milk
4 T yellow fat from chicken	1 cup chicken stock
stock	1 t lemon juice
6 T flour	

Mix flour with milk to thin paste. Bring chicken fat to boiling point, add milk mixture. Stir carefully until thick. Add chicken soup. Salt to taste and add lemon juice.

On a large platter arrange a bed of cooked rice. Place chicken on the rice and cover with the yellow sauce. Garnish with lemon slices and parsley. Button mushrooms and blanched almonds may be added to the yellow sauce.

CHICKEN BAKED IN SOUR CREAM
Kura Pieczona w Kwaśnej Śmietanie

1 roasting chicken	¾ cup sifted flour
1 egg	1 cup bread crumbs
3 T water	6 T butter
2 cups sour cream	Salt and pepper

Beat egg slightly and add cold water. Cut chicken in pieces. Dip in flour, egg and water, and dip in bread crumbs. Brown in butter. Remove to baking pan, sprinkle with salt and pepper and set in 375° oven. Heat sour cream to liquefy. After half hour of baking, pour a little hot sour cream over each piece. The cream will immediately soak into the chicken. In 15 minutes pour more sour cream and so on until all has been added. Bake chicken 1½ hours. The chicken will absorb all the cream.

To make gravy, remove chicken. Place 2 tablespoons of butter in roasting pan. Add 2 level tablespoons flour and mix until smooth. Add 2 cups milk. Stir constantly to dissolve all browned juice in pan. Allow to simmer 3 to 4 minutes.

This is a good way to cook game such as pheasant or young rabbit.

Kto prędko daje, dwa razy daje.
He who gives freely, gives twice.

CHICKEN WITH NOODLES
Potrawa z Drobiu z Łazankami

1 young hen   Chopped parsley
Egg Noodles (see page 28)

Cook chicken as for soup (see page 18). Make the noodles the day before. Dry them thoroughly. When chicken is tender, remove from soup. Strain soup. Do not remove any of the fat from the top because it imparts a rich flavor to the noodles. Cook noodles in the chicken soup. Place chicken in center of large platter and make a wide border of the noodles. Sprinkle with chopped parsley.

CHOPPED CHICKEN CUTLETS
Kotlety z Kury

1 soup chicken   1 t chopped chives
1 egg   Salt and pepper to taste

Cook chicken as above. Cool and remove from bones. Chop meat fine or run through meat grinder. Add egg, chives, and seasoning. Form into cutlets in the palm of your hand and fry quickly in butter until light brown.

STEWED CHICKEN
Kura Duszona

3 to 4 lbs. stewing chicken   2 stalks celery
Cold water   1 sprig parsley
2 onions, sliced   1 dry mushroom
1 carrot   Salt

Cut chicken at joints. Place in deep saucepan, add just enough cold water to cover it. Add other ingredients but not salt. Bring to boiling point, lower heat to simmering, and cook covered until tender. After an hour, add plenty of salt; it takes a lot to season the chicken properly. Cook for another one or two hours, depending upon the age of the chicken. It is done when the meat starts to fall away from the bones. If possible, cool chicken right in the cooking water; it will be more tender.

COQUILLES OF CHICKEN
Kokilki z Drobiu

2 cups cold cooked chicken   1 cup mushroom liquor
2 T butter   Salt and pepper
½ cup chopped mushrooms   ½ cup sherry
2 T flour   1 cup sweet cream
1 cup chicken broth

Saute mushrooms in butter. Thicken with flour and add chicken broth and mushroom liquor. Cook until smooth. Season and add sherry. When cold, add the cream and chicken. Fill ramekins or shells with chicken, dot with butter and sprinkle with buttered bread crumbs. Bake in 350° oven for 20 minutes.

60

JELLIED CHICKEN IN MAYONNAISE
Majonez z Kur

5 lbs. stewing chicken
2 cups chicken stock
2 cups mayonnaise
2 cups veal knuckle concentrate or
2 T gelatine, softened in ¼ cup cold water
Salt and pepper

1 t sugar
Juice of 1 lemon
¼ cup sliced olives
½ cup sliced sweet pickles
¼ cup sliced cooked carrot
¼ cup pickled mushrooms
¼ cup green capers
Thin slices of lemon

Cook the chicken according to directions for stewing chicken on page 18. Be sure to have 2 cups of stock when chicken is done. Cool chicken in stock. Remove meat from bones and leave in uniform large pieces. Stir the hot stock into the gelatine. Cool and add mayonnaise. Add chicken and other ingredients. Arrange a pattern with the pickles, carrots and mushrooms in bottom of a loaf pan. Pour the mixture into the pan and chill in refrigerator several hours or over night. Be sure to season this dish well. Unmold on bed of shredded lettuce and garnish with cold hard-cooked eggs, asparagus tips, and quartered beets.

CHICKEN LIVERS
Wątróbki z Kur

10 chicken livers
Milk
1 T butter
1 T flour
1 cup chicken broth

¼ cup Madeira wine
Flour for dredging
1 sliced onion
2 dry mushrooms
Salt

Soak liver in milk for 6 hours. Brown butter, add flour. Add the chicken broth and wine and mix until smooth. Dredge liver in flour and add to sauce. Add the onion and mushrooms. Cover and simmer for 15 minutes. Salt just before serving, because an earlier salting will toughen the livers.

GOOSE LIVER SPREAD
Wątróbka Gęsia

1 lb. young goose livers
½ lb. diced bacon
1 onion, chopped fine
2 T soup stock

2 T goose lard
Dash of nutmeg
Salt and pepper

Soak livers in milk over night. Fry onion with bacon until light brown. Run liver through food chopper. Add onion and soup stock. Add spices and goose lard. Mix thoroughly. Place in crock well rubbed with goose lard. Cover with muslin cloth dipped in salt water or egg white. Will keep indefinitely.

61

ROAST DUCK OR GOOSE WITH VARIED STUFFINGS
Pieczona Kaczka lub Gęś Nadziewana

Fowl   Salt and marjoram

If you are lucky to have a live duck or goose, save its blood in vinegar and salt for making **Czarnina** (page 22). Feather and clean the bird thoroughly. Use the feet, neck, wings, gizzard and heart for **Czarnina.** One hour before cooking rub the fowl inside and out with salt and marjoram. Fill with your favorite stuffing. Rub the skin with salt and pepper but no fat since the duck has enough of its own. The goose has so much that you must prick with a fork the legs and wings to let the fat run out during roasting. Roast in moderate oven for 35 minutes to the pound. The fat makes it self-basting; some of the fat should be poured off as it accumulates. For additional flavor, red wine or orange juice can be poured over the fowl several times.

Suggested Stuffings

Unpeeled apples, celery and onions
Sliced raw potatoes
Noodles and ham
Chestnuts

Sauerkraut sauteed in butter with chopped onion
Brown rice or wild rice and mushrooms

Chestnut Stuffing

Goose liver, chopped fine
1 large onion, chopped fine
Butter
2 lbs. chestnuts

3 apples, peeled, quartered
1/2 cup black raisins
Salt and pepper

Cook chestnuts in boiling water for 20 minutes, remove the shell and brown skin while hot, and grate. Fry liver in butter and onion. Mix all ingredients and stuff fowl.

Special Stuffing

Goose liver
1/2 lb. calf liver
1/2 lb. veal
1/2 lb. lean pork
1/2 lb. salt pork

2 egg yolks
6 slices dry white bread
1/2 t thyme
Salt and pepper

Run the first five ingredients through meat grinder twice. Slightly moisten the bread. Mix all ingredients well and stuff **fowl.**

62

STEWED DUCK OR GOOSE
Gęś lub Kaczka Duszona

Fowl
3 stalks celery
2 sprigs parsley
½ t marjoram
1 large onion

Salt and pepper
6 slices bacon
2 T butter
1 T flour
Water to cover

If the fowl is not young, salt the pieces of meat for one hour before cooking. Fry bacon, add vegetables, spices and fowl. At first let stew in its own juices; then add hot water, not much, just enough to keep from burning. Simmer slowly. At end of two hours when meat ought to be tender, remove from liquid. Brown flour in butter and stir into liquid to make gravy. Return meat to gravy, heat thoroughly. Serve with a garnish of chestnuts or vegetables.

STUFFED DUCK
Kaczki Faszerowane czyli Rolada

Ducks
Salt and pepper
½ lb. lean lamb
Onion, chopped
Butter
1 t bread crumbs

2 celery tops
1 parsley root
½ cup chopped mushrooms
6 sardines
¼ t lemon rind
3 eggs

Rub inside of duck with salt one hour before cooking. Split duck in half across back and remove the larger bones. Cook the lamb with gizzard, wings, neck and heart. Add celery tops, parsley root, onion and salt. Fry mushrooms in butter. Bone sardines. Chop meats and the mushrooms very fine. Add sardines, lemon rind, pepper, bread crumbs, and eggs. Mix well and fill the split duck. Tie securely with twine and place in pan. Add butter and chopped onion and simmer until tender. If juice cooks out, add stock from stuffing meats. Serve with caper or truffle sauce.

63

DUCK WITH RED CABBAGE
Kaczka Duszona z Kapustą

1 head red cabbage
1 onion
Salt
½ lb. salt pork

1 duck
½ cup red wine
Juice of 1 lemon

Shred cabbage coarsely. Chop onion. Salt cabbage and onion and let stand for 10 minutes. Squeeze out liquid. Cube salt pork and fry it. Add the cabbage and onion, the wine and lemon juice. Cover and simmer for 20 minutes. Brown the duck in the oven. Cut it at joints and cover cabbage with it. Season to taste. Cook until tender. Heap cabbage on platter and surround with duck.

LEG OF VENISON
Sarna Duszona

5 to 6 lbs. leg of venison
1 cup sour cream
1 cup red wine
½ cup butter
½ cup flour
2 or 3 lumps of sugar
1 onion
1 bunch of green onions
Few whole cloves
Salt and pepper to taste

Marinade:
1½ qts. white wine
2 cups vinegar
2 cups olive oil
¼ lb. sliced carrots
¼ lb. sliced onions
2 stalks celery
2 cloves garlic
3 sprigs parsley
1 bayleaf
Peppercorns
Few whole cloves

Soak the venison for 2 or 3 days in the marinade. Remove, wipe dry with a cloth. Melt the butter and brown the meat evenly on all sides. Fry the onion in the same butter, stir in one cup of the marinade, the red wine, and the sugar. Cover closely and simmer very gently for several hours till the meat is tender. Strain sauce, thicken with flour, and add the sour cream. Cut meat in slices and pour the sauce over them. Garnish with the green onions, lightly browned in butter. Boiled potatoes are often served with the dish.

POTTED PHEASANT
Bażant Pieczony

Pheasant
Flour for dredging
½ cup butter
1 onion
3 whole allspice

1 stalk celery
1 cup meat stock
1 cup cream
Salt and pepper
2 T sherry

Cut pheasant in desired pieces, roll in flour, and brown in butter. Add remaining ingredients. Bake in 350° oven for 1½ hours or until tender. Remove pheasant, strain the liquid. Add more cream, soup stock and the sherry. Thicken gravy. Serve with wild rice.

RABBIT
Zając Pieczony

Rabbit
Flour for dredging
4 T butter
1 onion, chopped
1 cup chopped mushrooms
1 clove garlic
3 pinches dry thyme
3 bay leaves
⅔ cup meat stock
⅔ cup tart white wine
Salt and pepper to taste

Cut rabbit in desired pieces, dredge with flour and brown in butter. Add rest of ingredients, bake in 350° oven until tender.

Should you not want to use wine, add 1 can cream of mushroom soup diluted with 1 cup water. This makes an excellent gravy.

PIGEONS
Potrawka z Gołębi

Pigeons
Butter
3 onions
1 cup meat stock
2 tart apples
3 mushrooms

Juice of ½ lemon
Small glass Madeira wine
1 T butter
1 T flour
1 cup sour cream

Quarter the pigeons. Saute in butter for 15 minutes. Remove from butter and slice three onions into pan. Fry onions until done. Add meat stock, sliced apples, mushrooms and lemon juice. Mix well and bring to boiling point. Add wine. In another pan brown flour in butter and thicken the mixture. Dip pigeons in sour cream, return to mixture and cook until tender. Pigeons may be fried or roasted like young chicken.

Głód wilka z lasu wyprowadzi.
Hunger will lead a fox out of the forest.

BIGOS

Every ancient Polish manor has its own cookery book, the growth of centuries; carefully bound, exquisitely-penned recipes, yellow with age. In those far-away times, when guests were awaited and some of those wonderful recipes were in course of realization, the cook was not grudged a bottle of good old honey wine to maintain him in a good humor or reproached if he used a pound or two of butter.

Among those recipes we should not fail to find one for **Bigos,** a most delectable dish served at every hunting party. In **Pan Tadeusz, Mickiewicz** said, "There has been a bearhunt. The bear is killed; a great fire is made and while the **Bigos** is warming in a mighty pot, the hungry hunters drink crystal clear, gold-flecked wodka from **Gdansk."**

Here it is:

Take a big head of hard white cabbage, slice it thinly, sprinkle with salt and let it stand an hour. Then press out the moisture. Chop finely two onions; dice some sour apples; cut into small pieces some fat boiled or roast beef and some uncooked pork (roast venison or game may be added if you have it). Mix together all these ingredients and put them in the sauce pan in the following manner: First a tablespoonful of butter, then a layer of the mixture, then another spoonful of butter and another layer, until all is in the saucepan. Pour over it some good stock, cover and simmer at least two hours, shaking the saucepan often to prevent burning. When the **Bigos** is nearly done, mix a spoonful of flour with a spoonful of melted butter, add it to the **Bigos,** stir well, let it simmer a little longer and it is ready to serve. **Bigos** thus prepared may be served as a luncheon dish or at dinner, before the soup. It may be warmed up—in fact it is even better so than when first served.

If sauerkraut is used (as it mostly is), it should first be covered with cold water, brought to the boil and the water drained off.

Note that the quantity of the meat to be used is left to the discretion of the cook. Any left-overs may be added and a glass or two of wine will enhance the flavor.

And here is a recipe for **Bigos** without cabbage:

Cut up any meat that you may have left over. Brown a spoonful of butter, add some meat or vegetable stock, a few diced apples, some onion, if liked, then the meat and a lump of sugar. Simmer gently until done.

BIGOS

½ lb. each of pork, veal, beef and lamb
½ lb. venison (optional)
1 large onion, chopped
½ lb. mushrooms, cooked
¼ lb. bacon
½ lb. Polish sausage, cut in small pieces
1 qt. sauerkraut
Water or vegetable stock
Salt and pepper

Wash sauerkraut and cook until tender. Cut bacon and fry. Add onion and meat and fry until meat is slightly brown. Add water or vegetable stock and cook until meat is tender. Add Polish sausage and sauerkraut and boil until the flavors blend. **Season to taste.**

FISH
RYBY

Fish, unlike meat, has very little connective tissue and what it has, softens quickly. Fish cooks in a short time and will fall apart if it is overcooked. Because of the lack of connective tissue you never have to worry about fish being tough. Most fish is cooked at high temperature. Long or slow cooking makes it dry. Fish is usually cooked in fat and is well browned to bring out the flavor and add richness. Sometimes it is boiled. Then the temperature should be barely simmering. Fish is at its tastiest when it is in season and is freshly caught. Just as important is the fact that fish is always most economical when in season. All fish calls for some kind of sauce, even if it is just melted butter with a little lemon juice, possibly seasoned with fresh herbs such as parsley, dill or chives. The more elaborate sauces go well with all but the most superior flavored fish.

An old Polish cook book warns that fish is very perishable and eating of spoiled fish will make you sick. It is best to buy it alive. Fresh fish is judged by the gills, which should be rosy red. The eyes should be clear, bright and bulging. The flesh should be firm and elastic and the odor fresh. Pickerel from the Vistula is good, but it is better from the River Lida. Those from Russia are dry and without flavor. Lake pike is good, others are bad. Those from the Vistula are good because you can usually get them alive.

The many fast days in the church calendar try the Polish housewife's skill with substitutions for meat. She serves fish and herring often. It is the basic food in the many-course Christmas Eve Supper.

BOILED NORTHERN PIKE WITH HORSERADISH SAUCE
Szczupak w Sosie Chrzanowym

3 lbs. pike	Salt and pepper
4 cups vegetable stock	Horseradish sauce
(page 24).	

68

Clean fish thoroughly and cut into 3 inch pieces. Pour cold stock over fish and simmer slowly for about half hour until tender. While cooking, add 1 tablespoon of cold water to the fish three times. Remove fish carefully to platter and cover with horseradish sauce. (Page 78).

CREAMED FISH
Ryby Duszone w Śmietanie

Fish, cut in pieces	½ cup cream
2 large onions, grated	Salt and pepper
¼ cup butter	Lemon juice

Rub pieces of fish with grated onion and saute in melted butter. Add cream and seasonings and cook 5 minutes. Serve with a sprinkle of lemon juice and garnish with lemon slices.

NORTHERN PIKE POLISH STYLE
Szczupak po Polsku

1 northern pike	10 peppercorns
4 cups water	2½ T lemon juice
1 carrot	Salt and pepper
1 onion	10 eggs
1 stalk celery	2 T butter

Add to water in a pan the carrot, onion, celery stalk, peppercorns and ½ tablespoon lemon juice. Salt well. Put the cleaned fish into the pan and boil for 30 minutes. Meanwhile boil the eggs and chop them well. Heat 2 tablespoons of butter in a skillet, add chopped eggs and 2 tablespoons of lemon juice. Salt and pepper to taste. When fish is cooked, take it from saucepan and pour egg sauce over the top. Serve with boiled potatoes.

PIKE IN WINE
Sandacz na Winie

2 lbs. pike fillets	Salt and pepper
1 cup white wine	

Place in saucepan the fish and wine and allow to simmer gently until tender. Season. Remove from pan and keep warm until sauce is made.

Sauce:	1 cup wine including juice
1½ T butter	of fish
1½ T flour	Salt and pepper
1 egg yolk, beaten	

Melt butter, add flour to make smooth paste. Add enough wine to the liquid in which fish was cooked to fill 1 cup. Add to butter and flour and cook over direct flame until the mixture thickens. Cool slightly and add egg yolk. Season to taste. Pour sauce over fillets and serve with slices of onion, boiled potatoes and garnish with parsley and lemon.

69

FRICASSEE OF PIKE
Fricassee z Sandacza

Pike
1 T butter
6 asparagus stalks
1 small cauliflower
6 mushrooms
1 cup water

1 T butter
1 T flour
1 T lemon juice
3 egg yolks
Salt and pepper

Cut fish in 3 inch pieces. Blanch vegetables. Cover bottom of pan with butter, vegetables and water. Over this place the fish and simmer slowly until tender. Carefully lift out fish and vegetables. Strain liquid and add to the creamed butter and flour to make sauce. When smooth, add 3 well beaten egg yolks. Heat but do not boil. Arrange fish in center of platter and cover with sauce. Garnish with vegetables.

NORTHERN PIKE WITH SAUCE
Szczupak z Polskim Sosem

1 northern pike
2 cups white wine
1 cup white vinegar
1/4 t saffron

1/2 cup seedless raisins
1 T butter
1 T flour
1 T sugar

Place fish in saucepan with wine, vinegar, saffron and raisins and simmer slowly for half hour. Cream flour with melted butter. When smooth add to liquid in saucepan and bring to boiling point. Carefully remove fish and serve with sauce.

CRAPPIES IN HORSERADISH
Karasie Duszone z Chrzanem

6 crappies
1/2 cup butter
1/4 cup horseradish

1/2 cup cream
Salt and pepper

Place a layer of fish in kettle. Cover with butter, horseradish and cream. Season to taste. Cover with another layer of fish and simmer gently until tender. It is inadvisable to cook more than two layers at one time. Do not overcook—crappies are tender.

CARP WITH SAUCE
Karp z Polskim Sosem

1 carp—1 onion—salt
Water enough to cover fish
1/2 cup vinegar
1 stalk celery
1 onion
2 sprigs parsley

10 peppercorns
1/4 cup raisins
1/4 cup chopped almonds
1/2 cup red wine
1 T lemon juice

Clean and cut fish into pieces. One hour before cooking, salt fish and alternate fish with slices of onion. Let stand one hour. Make stock of water and bouquet vegetables. Strain. Cook fish in stock until tender. This will take a very short time because carp is a soft fish. Remove fish and strain stock, to which add raisins, almonds, wine and lemon juice. If sauce is not an attractive dark color, add carmelized sugar. Serve fish garnished with roe and lemon slices.

FRIED FISH
Ryba Smażona

The flavor of all fried fish is enhanced by adding sliced raw onion to the cleaned salted fish. Fish should be salted for at least an hour before frying. An over night salting is better yet. Do not use the onion from the fish. If you must be careful with butter, it will be worth your while to save all week for Friday's fish. No other shortening can do for fish what butter does.

Pike, cut in pieces
Salt and pepper
1 onion, sliced
1 egg, slightly beaten
2 T water
Flour for dredging
1 cup bread crumbs
½ cup butter

Add onion to fish, salt and pepper, and keep in refrigerator over night. Wipe fish dry and dredge in flour. Thin egg with water. Dip fish in egg, roll in bread crumbs. Fry in butter until brown. Place in baking pan and bake about half hour in 350° oven. Garnish with lemon slices and parsley.

FRIED CRAPPIES WITH CREAM
Karasie Zapiekane w Śmietanie

6 crappies—salt—onion
½ cup butter
Flour for dredging
1 cup cream

1 T green dill, chopped
1 bouillon cube
1 T hot water

Salt fish, add onion and let stand at least 1 hour before cooking. Wipe dry, dredge in flour and fry in butter. When done, cover with dill. Dissolve bouillon cube in hot water, add to cream and pour over fish. Bake in 350° oven for 15 minutes.

PIKE IN BATTER
Sandacz Smażony w Cieście

Pike fillets, seasoned
Batter made as follows:
1 cup milk
1½ cups flour

2 t baking powder
1 egg
1 t butter
¼ t salt

Mix and sift dry ingredients. Add milk gradually and well beaten egg. Mix until smooth and add butter. Wipe fillets dry, dip in batter and fry in hot fat or friture. Cook until well browned. Serve with prune compote or caper sauce.

BAKED PIKE
Sandacz Pieczony

1 pike—salt—onion
½ cup melted butter
1 cup cream

1 cup white wine
Juice of 1 lemon

Salt fish, cover with onion slices and let stand at least one hour. Place in roasting pan and cover with cream, wine and lemon juice. Baste frequently. Bake at 350° for 30 to 45 minutes.

STUFFED BAKED FISH
Nadziewana Pieczona Ryba

1 pike or trout
Stuffing:
3 eggs
3 onions, chopped
3 apples, chopped
3 stalks celery, chopped

1½ lbs. dry bread
1 cup mushrooms
1 t sugar
½ t thyme
½ cup butter
Salt and pepper

Saute onion and celery in butter until yellow. Moisten bread and squeeze out water. Combine ingredients and mix thoroughly. Stuff the cleaned fish. Brush with butter and bake in 350° oven for one hour. Serve with any good sauce.

FISH PATTIES
Kotlety z Ryb

2 cups fish meat
2 slices dry bread
¼ cup milk
2 eggs
2 onions

Salt and pepper
Dash of ground mace
1 T butter
Bread crumbs
Butter for sauteing

Chop meat fine. Moisten bread with milk and squeeze dry. Fry onion in butter until transparent. Mix all ingredients thoroughly. Make cutlets in the palm of your hand. Dip in bread crumbs and saute in butter. Serve with tartar sauce or horseradish with whipped cream.

72

TROUT OR PIKE AU GRATIN
Pstrąg lub Szczupak Au Gratin

3 lbs. trout or pike
½ cup butter
½ cup bread crumbs
1 cup chopped mushrooms

1 small onion, chopped
1 cup grated Parmesan
  cheese
½ cup fish stock or water

Brush the grill with butter and sprinkle with bread crumbs. On this place the whole fish. Sprinkle generously with bread crumbs, the mushrooms and onion browned in butter, and the grated cheese. Dot generously with pieces of butter. Add stock. Bake in 350° oven for 45 minutes.

STUFFED PIKE GEFILLTE STYLE
Ryba Faszerowana po Żydowsku

3 lbs. northern pike
2 large onions
2 eggs, beaten
Salt and pepper

¾ cup bread crumbs
2 T chopped parsley
3 cups vegetable stock

Clean fish thoroughly and remove head. Cook head in vegetable stock for half hour. Pull skin off fish, being careful not to tear it. Remove meat from bones and put through grinder with the onions. Add eggs. Season highly with salt and pepper. Fill skin of fish with the ground mixture, making it look natural. The fish will be easier to handle if you sew it into a clean muslin cloth. Put into boiling stock and cook for about one hour.

FISH IN ASPIC
Ryba w Galarecie

3 lbs. pike
4 cups vegetable stock
  (page 24)
4 peppercorns
3 bay leaves

1 doz. capers
1 T gelatine
2 T water
1 egg white

Clean fish. Remove head and thoroughly clean it. Cook head and spices in vegetable stock for half hour. Strain. Place whole fish in pan. Cover with the strained stock and simmer for half hour until tender. Remove fish, cook stock. To clarify stock, add slightly beaten egg white and bring to boiling point, stirring lightly. Strain through napkin twice. Dissolve gelatin in water, add to stock. Pour over the cooled fish. Garnish with capers, carrot rings, hard-cooked eggs and lemon slices.

73

FISH DUMPLINGS
Pulpety z Ryb

3 lbs. fish meat
1 t salt
½ t ground pepper
1 onion, chopped
3 eggs, scrambled
Flour

2 slices dry bread
Milk to moisten bread
1 T butter
2 egg yolks
1 whole egg

Skin fish, remove bones and chop meat fine. Add other ingredients except flour and mix thoroughly. Sprinkle flour on work table, place mixture on flour and with floured spoon shape into balls. Drop into salted boiling water. As soon as dumplings rise to the top, remove from water and serve with fish soup.

CREAMED SHRIMP WITH RICE
Potrawka z Krewetków

3 cups cooked rice
2 cups cooked shrimp
2 T butter
2 T flour

.1 cup milk
1 t lemon juice
Salt and pepper
Chopped parsley

Melt butter, blend in flour and cook until mixture bubbles. Add milk gradually, stirring constantly until smooth. Reduce heat and cook for three minutes. Add lemon juice and seasoning. Add shrimp. Mound hot rice on large platter, cover with the creamed mixture. Garnish with parsley.

PICKLED HERRING
Śledzie Marynowane

3 whole salt herrings
2 large onions, sliced
1 cup vinegar

4 peppercorns
4 whole allspice
1 t sugar

Soak herrings in cold water for at least 24 hours. Change water every 8 hours or oftener. Save the milch from herrings. Skin, remove bones and cut each herring into 4 pieces. Arrange onions in a bed on a deep platter. Arrange herring on top of onions. Boil vinegar and cool. Rub milch through fine sieve, mix with vinegar and sugar and pour over the herring. Serve with whole boiled potatoes.

Łaknącemu wszystko smaczne.
A good appetite needs no sauce.

74

CHOPPED HERRING
Śledzie Siekane

2 fat salt herrings
3 hard cooked eggs

3 small onions
2 T sweet butter

Do not soak herring. Remove head, tail and skin from herring. Do not remove the bones. Chop herring, eggs and onion very fine. Add butter and mix well. Serve as spread on canapes or appetizers.

FRIED HERRING
Śledzie Smażone

3 salt herrings
1 egg
1 T water

Flour
Butter

Soak herrings for 24 hours. Clean herrings, remove head and tail but do not remove the skin. Cut herring in pieces. Thin egg with water. Dry herring with tissue, dip in flour, egg and in flour again. Fry quickly in butter, turning once.

HERRING PUDDING
Babka ze Śledzi

2 fat salt herrings
Milk
4 baked potatoes

1 egg
2 T sour cream
Dash of pepper

Soak herrings in milk for 18 hours. Remove meat from bones and chop fine. Peel hot baked potatoes and force through ricer. Mix with herring, add egg, and beat hard. Add sour cream and pepper. Bake in buttered casserole for 20 minutes in hot oven.

HERRING AND POTATO CASSEROLE
Śledzie Zapiekane z Kartoflami

5 medium potatoes
2 herrings
1 onion, chopped

2 t butter
1 cup cream

Soak herrings for 24 hours. Clean, remove meat from bones and chop coarsely. Cook potatoes in jackets until tender. While hot, peel and slice thin. Fry chopped onion in butter. In a buttered baking dish, alternate layers of potatoes, chopped herring and onion. Cover with cream. Sprinkle top with bread crumbs and melted butter. Bake. in 325° oven for one hour.

SAUCES
SOSY

All good cooking depends for its excellence on the quality of its sauces. A sauce by its special flavor or texture must complement and enhance the food with which it is served. Polish cuisine makes many and varied sauces, carefully seasoned with herbs grown in the garden and strengthened with stock and bones. The "sosjerka," sauce boat, is an important vessel on the Polish table. We list below only some of the simplest sauces.

BASIC WHITE SAUCE
Sos Biały

2 T butter
2 T flour
1 cup soup stock

4 T cream
Salt and pepper

Heat butter, blend in flour until smooth. Gradually add soup stock, stirring constantly. Bring to boiling point. Cook for three more minutes. Add cream and seasoning.

CAPER SAUCE
Sos Kaparowy

Add two tablespoons capers to each cup of white sauce.

DILL SAUCE
Sos Koperkowy

Add one tablespon fresh chopped dill to each cup of white sauce. Do not boil after addition of dill as it will lose its color and aroma.

PARSLEY SAUCE
Sos Pietruszkowy

Add two tablespoons minced parsley to each cup of white sauce.

YELLOW SAUCE
Sos z Jajami

Add hot white sauce to two slightly beaten egg yolks. Beat thoroughly.

76

MUSHROOM SAUCE
Sos Grzybowy

Add ½ cup chopped cooked mushrooms to each cup of white sauce.

SOUR CREAM SAUCE
Sos z Kwaśnej Śmietany

2 egg yolks	1 T minced parsley
¾ cup sour cream	½ t salt
1 T lemon juice	Paprika

Beat egg yolks, add sour cream and lemon juice. Heat in double boiler until thick and smooth. Season with salt and paprika and add the parsley. Serve over vegetables.

MUSHROOM SAUCE WITH WHITE WINE
Sos Grzybowy z Białem Winem

½ lb. fresh mushrooms	½ glass white wine
¼ lb. butter	2 egg yolks
Juice of ½ lemon	½ t salt
½ T flour	½ t sugar

Slice mushrooms, removing the stems. Cook stems in 1 cup of water and save the stock to use later. Melt in saucepan one-half the butter, add mushrooms and squeeze the lemon juice on the mushrooms. (No seeds). Add 3 tablespoons mushroom stock and cook slowly until mushrooms are soft. In another pan heat the other half of the butter and add flour. Add wine to mushroom stock, bring to boiling point and add mushrooms. Heat again and remove from fire. Mix some of the liquid with egg yolks and add very slowly to sauce. Season. Heat again, do not boil. Strain through sieve, add mushrooms and serve immediately. This can be made with canned mushrooms. Save juice for stock.

BECHAMEL SAUCE
Sos Beszamelowy

1 T butter	½ cup meat stock
2 T flour	½ t salt
1 cup milk	Dash of pepper

Melt butter, add flour and seasoning, stirring until well mixed. Add hot milk slowly, beat thoroughly. Add meat stock and continue beating until well mixed.

LEMON PARSLEY SAUCE
Sos Polski Zielony

2 T butter	1 T lemon juice
2 T flour	1 T minced parsley
1 cup boiling water	2 egg yolks
¼ t salt	Salt and pepper

Melt butter, add flour and gradually add water. Stir constantly until thick and smooth. Add lemon juice and parsley. Let cool slightly. Add beaten egg yolks and season. To avoid curdling do not allow sauce to boil after addition of egg yolks. Use for boiled vegetables.

BROWNED BUTTER
Masło Rumiane

3 T butter   2 T bread crumbs

Melt butter over low flame until it bubbles and becomes golden brown. Add bread crumbs and heat until bread crumbs are golden brown. Use as topping for vegetables.

HORSERADISH SAUCE
Sos Chrzanowy

2 T butter
1 T flour
½ cup vegetable stock
1 T grated horseradish

Juice of ½ lemon or
1 T vinegar
1 T minced parsley

Brown flour in butter, add vegetable stock, horseradish, and lemon juice. Bring to boiling point, add parsley. Serve hot.

ONION SAUCE
Sos Cebulowy

2 small onions
1 cup white sauce
  (see page 76)
Salt

1 t dry mustard
1 T vinegar
1 T sugar
2 T water

Chop onion fine. Cover with boiling water, let stand one hour. Drain and rub onion through sieve. Make white sauce, add onion. Add salt, mustard and vinegar. Carmelize sugar and water, add to sauce.

TOMATO SAUCE
Sos Pomidorowy

2 T butter
1 T flour
½ cup meat stock

1 onion chopped fine
3 or 4 tomatoes, chopped
Sugar (optional)

Melt one tablespoon butter, add flour. When it bubbles, add the meat stock. Simmer tomatoes and onion in the other tablespoon butter for ten minutes. Rub through sieve, add to the flour mixture. Salt to taste. Add sugar if desired.

FRESH MUSHROOM SAUCE
Sos z Grzybków Świeżych

½ lb. fresh mushrooms
1 T and 1 t butter
1 small onion, chopped fine
2 T minced parsley

1 T flour
½ cup meat stock
½ cup sour cream
Salt

78

Wash and cut mushrooms into small pieces. Melt the table-spoon butter, add onion, mushrooms and parsley. Cook until tender, about 20 minutes. Blend flour with meat stock, add to mushrooms. Add cream, salt to taste. Add the remaining tea-spoon of butter. Dry mushrooms may be used, but they must be cooked first.

RAISIN SAUCE FOR TONGUE
Sos Słodki z Rodzynkami do Ozoru

1 T flour	2 t sugar
1 T butter	2 t water
1 cup soup stock or bouillon	½ cup raisins
1 cup wine	2 T hot vinegar

Melt butter, blend in flour. Add soup stock and wine, bring to boil. Carmelize sugar and water. Add to sauce. Add raisins and hot vinegar. Bring to boil again. Use honey instead of sugar, if you have it.

MAYONNAISE—1
Majonez

1 egg yolk, cooked	Juice of one lemon
1 egg yolk, uncooked	½ t salt
1 cup salad oil	

Rub the cooked yolk through a sieve. Add raw yolk. Beat thoroughly. (Be sure the yolk is free of all white.) Add oil drop by drop, beating constantly. This mixture should be thick and creamy. Add salt and lemon juice after you have added about three tablespoons of oil. Tarragon vinegar may be used for an interesting flavor.

MAYONNAISE—2
Majonez, 2gi Sposób

8 egg yolks
8 T cream
1 T vinegar
8 T salad oil
Salt
(Capers and dry mustard
    optional)

Combine yolks (free of any whites), salad oil, cream and vinegar in top of double boiler, over heat, and beat to a white foam. Cool. Add salt to taste. Add a little mustard and a few chopped capers if you like.

MAYONNAISE—3
Majonez, 3ci Sposób

4 egg yolks
Salt
1 cup olive oil

1 T lemon juice
1½ cups cold veal or fish stock
1 T gelatine

Beat egg yolks and salt. Add salad oil drop by drop. Beat well. Add lemon juice. Gradually add gelatine dissolved in stock.

TARTAR SAUCE
Sos Tatarski

1 cup mayonnaise
1 t chopped chives or onions
1 T capers

2 T chopped sweet pickles
1 T lemon juice

Combine all ingredients and mix well. Chill before using.

FRESH HORSERADISH
Chrzan Surowy

2 or 3 horseradish roots
Tarragon vinegar

Sugar to taste

Grate the horseradish. Set in warm place and let stand one hour. Put in jar, cover with vinegar. Add sugar. The horseradish with vinegar will keep a long time if sugar is omitted.

FRESH HORSERADISH WITH CREAM
Chrzan ze Śmietaną

½ cup grated horseradish
    root
½ cup sweet cream

1 t sugar
1 T vinegar or lemon juice

Scrape and grate horseradish root and let stand one hour. Add cream and sugar and mix well. Add vinegar or lemon juice. Serve with fish, boiled beef or ham.

FLUFFY HORSERADISH SAUCE
Chrzan z Bitą Śmietaną

1 cup horseradish
1 cup whipped cream

Dash of ground pepper

Fold horseradish into whipped cream, add pepper.

CHEESE SAUCE
Sos z Twarożkiem

1 cup sour cream
3 T horseradish

1 cup cottage cheese

Whip 1 cup sour cream and add horseradish. Mix with cottage cheese. Serve on raw vegetables.

~~~~~~

Kto nie dłużny ten bogaty.
He is rich who owes nothing.

HARD SAUCE
Sos Szodonowy

½ cup sugar   1 cup white wine
5 egg yolks

Beat eggs and sugar until thick and lemon colored. Add wine and mix thoroughly. Place over very low flame and continue beating until thick. Serve with hot desserts.

CREAM SAUCE
Sos Śmietankowy

3 egg yolks   1 t vanilla
½ cup sugar   1 cup scalded milk

Beat eggs, add sugar and vanilla. Gradually add milk. Heat over low flame. Do not boil. Serve hot or cold with puddings.

FRUIT JUICE SAUCE
Sos z Soków

1½ cup water   ½ cup sugar
1 cup fruit juice   1 t potato flour or corn starch

Bring water and fruit juice to boil. Add sugar. Blend the flour with a little water. Add to juice mixture. Bring to boil, stirring constantly. Serve with hot desserts. Half a cup of wine may be added if desired, then add a little more potato flour.

~~~~~~

BLACK MADONNA*

We are the stranger sons,
the prodigals, we have returned.
We are the lonely ones
who always sought for you and yearned.

We found the ancient gate,
the ancient house our people fled,
and friendly hands that wait
to serve us wine and salt and bread.

And what we have endured:
that hunger in our hearts since birth,
their smiles and words have cured.
O Black Madonna bless their hearth!

       —Alan Edward Symanski
"Against Death in the Spring," 1934
From Anthology of Polish-American Poetry, 1937
*Matka Boska Częstochowska

VEGETABLES
JARZYNY

STANLEY LEGUN

Farming was the chief source of food for the Polish folk. The crops raised were: rye, barley, millet, buckwheat and maize, potatoes, beets, onions, radishes, turnips, kohlrabi, beans, peas, lentils, cabbages and cucumbers. Poppies were grown for their seeds and oil; hemp and sunflowers also provided cooking oils.

Our Polish immigrants who settled in the cities always provided for their winter supply by buying sacks and sacks of potatoes, dozens of heads of cabbage, a couple of sacks of onions, peas, carrots, rutabagas and navy beans. In Poland they raised these vegetables on their small plots of ground. It is no wonder they have developed many tasteful ways of preparing them.

* * *

Long before cook books were written, when women cooked by instinct only, they established certain fundamental rules in cooking vegetables. The passing of time has not altered these rules. There is a harmony in all of nature.

Vegetables that grow underground in the cold earth, should always start cooking in cold water. Hot water will shock them, toughen fibers in some, and will not bring out the flavor. Always cover the kettle with a lid. Do not boil too rapidly. Potatoes cooked at a full rolling boil will have hard centers. Did you ever mash potatoes very earnestly and continue to find hard little lumps in them? They are the hard centers caused by boiling too rapidly.

Vegetables that grow above the surface of the earth should start cooking in boiling water. They have been warmed by the hot sun and yield to heat. Never cover them in the cooking. Most of these vegetables are green and the steam under the cover will affect the color. Fresh, green vegetables require less water than others. Strong flavored vegetables like cabbage, cauliflower, onions and turnips should be cooked in a large amount of water. Always salt vegetables in cooking, except fresh peas. No amount of salting at the table will give them the right flavor.

Cooking vegetables is not as difficult as preparing meats and other dishes. Yet, they too require deft handling. Do not keep too long in water before cooking, do not overcook, and do not let them lounge in kettles after they are cooked. They must be drained as soon as tender and served immediately.

82

ASPARAGUS
Szparagy

1 lb. asparagus	½ t sugar
Boiling water	2 T butter
1 T salt to quart of water	2 T bread crumbs

Break off the tough end of the stalk. With a knife scrape the lower half of each stalk. Tie asparagus into bundle and stand upright in cooking vessel. Cover with boiling water and boil 5 minutes. Drain off all this water and refill pot with boiling water. Add salt and sugar and cook uncovered until tender, about 20 minutes. Carefully lift asparagus to serving dish. Lightly brown bread crumbs in hot butter and pour over asparagus. For variety, chop hard-cooked eggs and parsley. Mix and sprinkle over buttered asparagus.

To freshen wilted asparagus, cover with muslin cloth and bury in the ground for 12 to 42 hours.

ASPARAGUS WITH SOUR CREAM
Szparagy z Kwaśną Śmietaną

Arrange cooked asparagus in a shallow buttered baking dish. Cover with ½ cup sour cream. Sprinkle with ½ cup bread crumbs browned in butter and bake at 350° until brown.

ASPARAGUS WITH PARMESAN
Szparagi z Parmezanem

On round serving dish, arrange cooked asparagus in circle, stalks radiating from center. Sprinkle with Parmesan cheese. Over the top pour melted butter and croutons.

GREEN BEANS
Groch Szparagowy

1 lb. young green beans	1 T butter or
Boiling water	3 slices crisp bacon
Salt and pepper	1 small onion, chopped

Cook beans in boiling water for 5 minutes. Drain and cover with fresh boiling water. Salt and cook uncovered until tender, about 15 minutes. In the last 5 minutes of cooking, add butter or diced bacon with onion.

BEETS
Buraki

6 medium sized beets	1 cup sweet cream
2 T butter	1 T lemon juice (optional)
1 T flour	

Boil beets until tender. Peel and grate. Brown butter and flour, add to beets. Add cream and cook for three minutes, stirring constantly. For tartness, add lemon juice.

BEETS
Buraki

6 cooked beets	1 T vinegar
2 T butter	½ t salt
1 T flour	½ cup sour cream
1 T granulated sugar	¼ t caraway seeds

Peel and grate cooked beets. Melt butter, add flour and bring to boiling point. Add vinegar, salt, sugar and caraway seeds. Mix with beets and boil for 2 or 3 minutes. Add sour cream, heat and serve.

PICKLED BEETS
Ćwikła

10 medium sized beets	1 T salt
1 T grated horseradish	1 t sugar
5 whole cloves or	2 cups vinegar
¼ t caraway seed	

Cook beets until tender. Slip off skins by holding under cold running water. Cut into thin slices. In glass or earthenware bowl, arrange layers of beets and sprinkle with horseradish and spices. Boil the vinegar, salt and sugar and pour over the beets. Let stand 24 hours.

Except in soups, beets should be cooked in their skins. Peeling or breaking a skin in cooking, will let the sugar juices escape.

BRUSSELS SPROUTS
Kapusta Brukselka

1 lb. brussels sprouts	Salt and pepper
Boiling water	2 T butter
Scalded milk	2 T bread crumbs

Pull off wilted leaves and cut stems close to the sprout. Wash and leave whole. Soak for half hour in cold salted water to draw out any insects. Drain well before cooking. Place in kettle and cover with boiling water. Cook for five minutes uncovered. Drain water and cover with scalded milk. Salt, pepper and cook uncovered until tender when pierced with fork. There should be very little milk left at end of cooking period. Serve with browned crumbs.

CABBAGE IN SOUR CREAM
Kapusta ze Śmietaną

1 small tender head cabbage	1 cup sour cream
½ cup butter	2 T sugar
Salt and pepper	2 T lemon juice
1 egg, beaten	

84

Cut cabbage fine. Saute in butter until tender but not brown. Season. Mix egg, cream, sugar and lemon juice. Pour over the cooked cabbage, toss lightly and heat thoroughly but do not boil.

SWEET SOUR CABBAGE
Kapusta Świeża na Kwaśno

1 medium head cabbage	2 T butter or
2 onions	4 slices bacon
2 T vinegar	1 T flour
2 tart apples	1 T sugar
	Salt and pepper

Shred cabbage, chop onion and combine. Cover with 2 tablespoons of salt and let stand one hour. Squeeze out liquid and cover with boiling water. Let stand 10 minutes and drain. Cover with boiling water and cook with apples, sugar and vinegar until tender. Make roux of butter or bacon fat, flour and one cup of cabbage liquid. Add to cabbage with chopped bacon.

CABBAGE WITH APPLES
Kapusta z Jabłkamy

1 medium head cabbage	1 t sugar
1 T salt	1 T butter or
3 or 4 green apples	3 slices crisp bacon
2 tomatoes (optional)	2 sliced onions

Shred cabbage. Cover cabbage and onion with boiling water. Let stand 10 minutes. Place butter or broken bacon slices in bottom of kettle. Add drained cabbage with onion, apples and tomatoes. Remove seeds from tomatoes. Seeds will give a bitter taste to the cabbage. Add sugar and simmer until tender, about 20 minutes. Salt during cooking.

RED CABBAGE
Kapusta Czerwona

1 medium head red cabbage	1 t sugar
1 T salt	Dash of pepper
1 cup red wine	Dash of ground cloves
1 T butter	1 T vinegar
1 T flour	

Shred cabbage, cover with salt and let stand 10 minutes. Drain the liquid. Cover cabbage with boiling water and cook until tender. When nearly done, add wine, sugar and spices. Brown butter, blend in flour and add 1 cup cabbage liquid. If wine is not sour, add vinegar for tartness. Cook until smooth and mix with cabbage. Serve with steak or game.

YOUNG CARROTS
Marchewka

8 to 10 small carrots　　　　1 t sugar
1 cup water　　　　　　　　2 T butter
Salt to taste

Scrub and scrape carrots. Leave them whole or cut into quarters, dice or thin strips. Cook slowly in a small amount of cold water with salt, sugar and butter. Cook until carrots absorb all the liquid. Watch closely.

WHOLE YOUNG CARROTS
Marchewka Drobna w Całości

12 young carrots　　　　　1 cup meat stock
1 T butter　　　　　　　　2 egg yolks
1 T sugar　　　　　　　　Salt

Scrub and scrape carrots. Melt butter in kettle, add carrots, sugar, salt and meat stock. Cook covered until tender. Beat egg yolks and add to carrots. Heat through but do not boil.

SLICED CARROTS
Marchew Krajana

8 carrots, sliced　　　　　2 T sugar
Water to cover　　　　　　1 T butter
Salt　　　　　　　　　　　1 T flour
½ cup meat stock

Cover carrots with water. Add salt, sugar and cook until tender. Heat butter, blend in flour and thin with meat stock. Add to carrots and mix thoroughly. Serve with cutlets or roasts. On a fast day, serve with croutons.

CAULIFLOWER
Kalafior

1 cauliflower, 2 to 3 lbs.　　　2 hard-cooked eggs
1 T vinegar　　　　　　　　1 t parsley
3 T butter　　　　　　　　　Salt
½ cup bread crumbs　　　　　Dash of nutmeg

Soak cauliflower, head down, in cold water with vinegar for about half hour to draw out any insects. Drain well before cooking. Place in boiling water and cook for 5 minutes. Drain. Cover with fresh boiling water and cook about 25 minutes until tender. Salt during cooking. Do not over-cook. When done, lift out carefully and cover with bread crumbs browned in the melted butter. Chop eggs and sprinkle over cauliflower with parsley and nutmeg.

~~~~~~

Rzucać groch o ściane.
Throw peas against a wall: Water on a duck's back.

86

CAULIFLOWER WITH CHEESE
Kalafior ze Serem

1 cauliflower
1 T vinegar
½ cup melted butter
Salt

1 cup Bechamel Sauce
(page 77)
½ cup Parmesan cheese
½ cup bread crumbs

Cook cauliflower as above. Place in casserole. Sprinkle with grated Parmesan cheese. Cover with Bechamel sauce. Mix remaining cheese with bread crumbs and sprinkle over sauce. Pour butter generously over all and bake in oven for 15 minutes at 350° until the cheese melts and blends with sauce.

CORN
Kukurydza

An old Polish cook book says simply: Select ears that are not too young and not too old. Boil in salted water with teaspoon of sugar for 15 minutes. Pass with it the butter dish and the salt shaker.

CUCUMBERS WITH SOUR CREAM DRESSING
Mizeria

2 large cucumbers
Boiling water to cover
½ cup sour cream
1 t salt
1 t sugar

Dash of pepper
1 t chopped dill, optional
1 t chopped chives, optional
1 hard-cooked egg, optional
Lemon juice or vinegar

Wash cucumbers. If they are young with a tender skin and from your garden, do not peel them. Peel others and run a fork lengthwise down the cucumber to a depth of ⅛ inch to make a scallop on each slice. Slice the cucumber so thin that you can see the knife through it while you are slicing. Cover with boiling water and let stand 10 minutes. Drain and plunge cucumbers into cold water. Drain and set in refrigerator for half hour. Mix sour cream with sugar, pepper and any of the optional ingredients. Salt cucumbers well and combine with sour cream mixture. Correct the tartness with lemon juice or vinegar. Serve cold.

Salting cucumbers to wilt them, makes them indigestible. They have a way of reminding you all afternoon that you had them for lunch. Scalding will wilt them and remove the bitterness.

STUFFED CUCUMBERS
Ogórki Faszerowane

6 medium cucumbers
1 cup ground veal
1/4 cup chopped onion
1/4 cup chopped mushrooms

Salt and pepper
2 eggs
1 cup bread crumbs
Butter

Peel cucumbers and cut in half lengthwise. Scoop out seed section carefully. Scald with boiling water and drain. Fry onion with butter, add mushrooms. Add chopped meat, 1 beaten egg and seasoning. Fill cucumber shells and tie halves together with thread. Simmer in water or meat stock until tender. Drain. Dip in slightly beaten egg, the crumbs and fry in butter until brown.

CELERY WITH WINE
Selery z Winem

1 bunch celery
Meat stock or water
Salt
1 t sugar

2 T butter
2 T flour
1 jigger Madeira wine

Cut leaves, wash and dry for use in soup bouquets. Pull the stalks apart and wash well. Scrape off the strings and cut into pieces. Place in kettle and cover with meat stock or water. Add salt and sugar and cook until tender, about 15 minutes. Heat butter, add flour and when blended, add wine. Add to celery and bring to a boil. Very tasty with poultry.

WILTED LEAF LETTUCE
Sałata Laktuka

Leaf lettuce
4 slices bacon, diced
1/4 cup water
Salt and pepper

1/4 cup **vinegar**
1 t shallots or onion, chopped
3 T sugar

Wash lettuce thoroughly, dry, and cut coarsely. Add shallots, sugar, salt and pepper. Fry bacon until golden brown. Dice it and add to lettuce. Into 2 tablespoons hot bacon fat, add the vinegar and water and bring to a boil. Pour over lettuce, mix and serve.

TOSSED HEAD LETTUCE
Sałata ze Śmietaną

1 head lettuce
1 cup sour cream
3 hard-cooked eggs
Salt

1 T mayonnaise
1 T lemon juice or vinegar
1 T sugar

Wash, dry and separate the head of lettuce. Break leaves into small pieces. Mash hard-cooked egg yolks with a fork. Add mayonnaise, salt and sugar and beat well. Add sour cream and lemon juice. Mix thoroughly. Add chopped egg whites. Pour over the lettuce and toss with a fork.

88

ONIONS
Cebula

There are four main types of onions: white, red, yellow and Bermuda. The white onions are smallest and mild in flavor. Yellow onions are larger and have a stronger flavor. Red onions are about the same size and are similar in flavor. Bermuda are the largest of all and have a mild sweet flavor. Polish recipes say "No good cook would use onions without scalding them first."

Dean Swift says:
This is every cook's opinion
No savory dish without an onion,
But lest your kissing should be spoil'd,
Your onions must be thoroughly boil'd.

PARSNIP
Pasternak

Parsnips	Melted butter or
Boiling salted water	Small piece pork or lamb

Wash and peel. Cut into lengthwise strips. Cut out the cores if they seem tough. Cook in boiling salted water until tender, about 20 to 30 minutes. Add 1 tablespoon of butter to water. Drain well and serve with melted butter. For a richer flavor, cook them with a piece of pork or lamb. Parsnip adds a distinct flavor to soup bouquet vegetables.

PARSLEY
Pietruszka

Every little garden in Poland grows parsley. It is used primarily for garnish. Parsley root adds zestive flavor to soups and stews. Polish cooks dry bunches of parsley to tide them over the winter until next season's planting. Some recipes call for fried parsley: just drop it into hot butter or friture until it is crisp. You can dip in egg and bread crumbs and then fry.

PEAS
Groszek Zielony

2 cups shelled green peas	1 t sugar
Water to cover	1 T butter
Salt	1 T flour

Cover peas with water, add sugar and cook about 20 minutes until tender. Do not add salt while they are cooking because salt makes them tough. Cook uncovered to preserve color. There should be very little water left in the saucepan. Heat butter, blend in flour and add to peas. Salt to taste.

GREEN PEAS IN POD
Groszek w Strączkach

1 lb. very young green peas   1 t salt
  in pod   1 t sugar
1 T butter

Wash peas and trim ends. Barely cover with water and cook for 10 minutes. Add salt and sugar and continue cooking until tender, about 15 to 20 minutes more. Melt butter and pour over peas.

GREEN PEAS WITH MUSHROOMS
Groszek z Grzybami

2 cups shelled fresh peas   ½ cup cooked mushrooms,
1 t salt   chopped
2 T butter

Shell peas. Boil in small amount of water until tender. Salt and drain. Saute mushrooms in butter. Add to peas and mix.

GREEN PEAS AND NEW POTATOES
Groszek z Kartofelkami

2 cups small new potatoes   1 cup sweet or sour cream
2 cups shelled green peas   1 t chopped parsley
Salt and pepper   Dash of paprika
1 T melted butter

Use tiny new potatoes or cut large potatoes into balls with a vegetable scoop. Cook potatoes for about 20 minutes until tender in boiling salted water. Cook peas separately for 10 to 15 minutes. Drain, add salt and pepper. Combine vegetables and pour the cream over them. Add parsley and paprika and when hot, serve at once.

GREEN PEAS WITH RICE
Groszek z Ryżem

½ cup rice
2 cups shelled green peas
½ cup chopped mushrooms
1 small onion, chopped
3 T butter
1 T Parmesan cheese

Boil rice in 2 quarts of salted water. Drain and rinse rice with hot water. Cook green peas in a small quantity of water for 10 to 15 minutes. Fry onion in butter, add mushrooms and fry for 10 minutes. Combine ingredients and bake in casserole for 30 minutes at 350°. Sprinkle top with Parmesan cheese and buttered bread crumbs before baking.

RUTABAGA
Brukiew

1 rutabaga	1 T butter
Chicken or goose stock	1 T flour
1 T sugar	Salt

Pare and dice rutabaga. For best flavored rutabagas cook them in chicken stock or stock made of goose neck, wing tips, gizzard, heart and feet. A young rutabaga should be tender in 20 minutes. Add sugar while it is cooking. At end of cooking period, there should be only a small amount of liquid. Brown butter, add flour and thin with 3 tablespoons of rutabaga liquid. Add to rutabaga, heat, and serve.

RUTABAGA AND CARROT BALLS
Brukiew z Marchwią

2 cups rutabaga balls	1 T flour
2 cups carrot balls	1 T butter
Meat stock	1 t dill or parsley
1 T sugar	Salt

Cut balls with a vegetable scoop. If you do not have meat stock on hand, cook a small piece of pork for stock. Add the vegetables, sugar and salt. Cook until tender. Brown butter, add flour and make roux with 3 tablespoons of vegetable liquid. When smooth, add to vegetables. Garnish with chopped dill or parsley.

KOHLRABI
Kalarepa

6 kohlrabi	1 T butter
Salt	1 T flour
1 T butter	1 T cream
1 T sugar	

Use only tender young vegetables. Peel and cut into thin slices or dice. Cook in water with 1 tablespoon butter, salt and sugar, until tender. Heat butter, blend in flour and add cream. Mix with kohlrabi and serve at once.

PUMPKIN
Dynia albo Bania

1 small pumpkin	2 cups egg barley
Salt	1 T sugar
2 qts. milk	$\frac{1}{2}$ t ground cinnamon

Peel and dice pumpkin. Cook in small amount of salted water until tender. Mash through sieve. Cook milk with egg barley (page 30), add pumpkin, sugar and cinnamon. Serve with Lenten meals.

SPINACH
Szpinak

2 lbs. spinach
Salt
½ cup cream

3 T butter
1 t flour

Always wash spinach in lukewarm water and lift it out of the water rather than drain spinach and water through sieve. Drain water from pan, fill with fresh cold water and put spinach back. Repeat this process two or three times until the water in the bottom of the pan stays clean. Leave spinach in last water for 10 to 20 minutes to soak out the remaining bits of dirt. Cook in boiling salted water, allowing it to turn over a few times. Rinse in cold water and drain. Chop. Heat butter, add flour and cream and add to spinach. Heat but do not boil or it will lose color. Garnish with buttered croutons or chopped hard-cooked eggs.

SPINACH
Szpinak

2 lbs. spinach
4 slices bacon
1 T flour
½ t sugar
½ cup cream

Grating of lemon peel
Dash of mace
Salt and pepper
Croutons

This spinach must be young. Cook spinach with no water except what drips from the leaves, and let it remain there steaming only until the leaves are well wilted. Fry bacon crisp, chop and add to spinach. Mix flour, sugar, cream, salt and pepper, grating of lemon peel and mace separately. Add this sauce to chopped spinach, beating it in well. Heat in oven and serve with croutons.

POTATOES
Kartofle - Ziemniaki - Ziemiaki

Potatoes play a very important part in the diet of the Poles. They are eaten in some form every day. Polish cooks serve them in many variations.

NEW POTATOES
Młode Kartofelki

New potatoes
Boiling salted water

1 T butter
1 t chopped dill

They are a rare delicacy when properly prepared. Scrape the potatoes. Wash well. Cover with hot water, salt and cook covered on medium heat until tender. Drain and add butter and dill.

Miłość karmi się nadzieją.
Hope keeps love alive.

BOILED POTATOES
Kartofle Gotowane

Potatoes   Cold water   Salt

Peel potatoes. Cover with cold water and set on hot fire. When they reach boiling point, add salt, remove scum, cover and boil slowly until tender, about half hour. The quantity and size of potatoes determines the cooking time. Drain, cover and put back on slow fire. Gently shake pot over the flame, raising the lid to allow steam to escape freely. This will dry and make the potatoes mealy. If you decide to flavor potatoes with buttered bread crumbs or chopped crisp bacon or chopped onion, butter and chopped dill, add to potatoes immediately after draining, mix well and remove cover. Serve boiled potatoes at once. In the spring when potatoes reach their cycle of life and are ready to enter the earth again, their flavor spoils. Then cover potatoes with boiling water, boil 5 minutes, drain and pour fresh boiling water over them and cook.

POTATOES AND MUSHROOMS
Kartofle i Grzyby

Small new potatoes	1 cup meat stock
1/4 cup butter	2 egg yolks
2 T green onions or chives	1 t white wine or lemon juice
1/2 lb. mushrooms, chopped	Salt and pepper

Cook new potatoes until tender. Drain and dry. Place in casserole, adding butter and chopped onion. Add mushrooms and stock to which you have added the egg yolks diluted with wine or lemon juice. Season. Bake 30 minutes in 350° oven.

BOILED POTATOES IN JACKETS
Kartofle w Mundurach

Medium sized potatoes	Boiling water
Salt	Butter

Wash potatoes with brush and rinse in several waters. Cover with boiling water and let stand for 10 minutes. Drain water. Place potatoes in kettle, cover with boiling water, add salt and bring to a boil rapidly. Reduce heat and boil until tender. Drain, remove cover and return to fire to allow steam to escape. Serve immediately with butter and salt.

BAKED POTATOES
Kartofle Pieczone

Select uniform potatoes. Clean with brush and rinse several times. Dry them. Rub skin with bacon fat and bake in 450 degree oven for about 45 minutes. They are delicious when baked with rye flour. Sprinkle a generous layer of rye flour into baking pan. Arrange dry potatoes on flour and cover thickly with rye flour. Serve with butter, salt and pepper.

93

POTATO BALLS
Drobne Kartofelki Smażone

Peel potatoes. Make small balls 1 inch in diameter with vegetable scoop. Add salt and bit of sugar to flour. Dredge in flour, throw into hot butter and cook until done. They are a golden-brown and look candied. Serve with steak.

POTATO BALLS
Kotleciki z Kartofli

6 potatoes, mashed
½ cup flour
3 egg yolks

¼ t celery seed
Salt and pepper
Egg yolk and bread crumbs

Cook and mash potatoes. When cool, add other ingredients, mix well and shape into small balls with the hands. Dip into egg yolk and crumbs. Fry in butter, deep fat or bake in oven to the right color and crispness.

WHIPPED POTATOES
Kartofle Tłuczone

2 qts. boiled potatoes, hot
1 T butter

1 cup sweet cream

Mash potatoes thoroughly. Add butter and cream and beat until they are white and fluffy. This is best done over boiling water.

WHIPPED POTATOES IN THREE COLORS
Eleganckie Puree w Trzech Kolorach

Divide above recipe into four parts. To one, add cooked spinach; to the other, add tomato paste; cover the third with buttered bread crumbs and leave the fourth natural. Serve in round shallow dish, arranging potatoes in shape of star. In center place bouquet of parsley and border with croutons. A nourishing Lenten dish.

POTATO SOUFFLE
Suflet z Kartofli

3 cups mashed potatoes
3 eggs, separated
Bread crumbs

Melted butter
Chopped parsley
Salt and pepper

Add yolks to potatoes and beat hard. Correct seasoning. Beat whites and fold into potatoes. Place in casserole, sprinkle with parsley and bread crumbs, and pour butter over top. Bake in 350° oven for 30 minutes. Serve with fish and chops.

94

FRENCH FRIES
Kartofle Chrupiące

Potatoes cut in desired pieces   Salt or garlic salt
Friture for frying (page 42)

Peel and cut potatoes. Soak for half hour in cold water to remove starch. Wipe dry. Fry in deep hot fat until yellow. Remove from fat, cool for 5 minutes. Return to hot fat and brown. The interrupted cooking makes them light, dry and puffs them. Sometime try garlic salt on them.

STUFFED POTATOES
Kartofle Nadziewane

6 large unmarked potatoes   1 cup chopped mushrooms
3 T butter   ¼ cup bread crumbs
1 onion, chopped fine   2 egg yolks
Salt and pepper

Peel potatoes and place in baking dish, whole. Bake in 350° oven for 30 minutes. Cut off cap at top of potato. Scoop out center and fill with mushroom mixture made as follows: Fry onion and mushrooms in butter for 10 minutes. Add bread crumbs, egg yolks and seasoning. Fill potatoes, replace cap and return to buttered baking dish, cap side up. Bake for half hour at 350°. You may vary the stuffing with ground ham, ground cooked meat, riced potatoes.

POTATOES WITH HAM
Kartofle z Szynką

3 cups mashed potatoes, hot   2 cups diced ham
1 cup sour cream   2 egg whites
2 egg yolks   Salt and pepper

Beat egg yolks with potatoes. Season and add sour cream and diced ham. Beat egg whites and fold into potatoes. Place in buttered casserole, dot with butter and bake for half hour at 350°.

ROYAL POTATOES WITH CHEESE
Kartofle Książęce z Serem

4 cups sliced boiled potatoes   Salt
2 cups grated cheese   3 eggs
Butter   3 cups milk

Peel and slice potatoes while they are hot. Butter a casserole and arrange layer of potatoes, sprinkle with cheese and melted butter, until all are used up. Beat eggs with milk, add salt, and pour over the potaotes. Bake 1 hour at 350°.

POTATOES WITH EGGS AND CREAM
Kartofle Zapiekane ze Śmietaną

3 cups diced cooked potatoes
1 T butter
Salt and pepper

2 eggs, beaten
1 cup sour cream
1 T chopped chives

Melt butter in frying pan and saute potatoes until they are thoroughly heated. Salt and pepper to taste. Add sour cream, eggs and chives. Bake covered in 350° oven for one hour.

ESCALLOPED POTATOES
Kartofle Duszone Wyborne

4 cups sliced raw potatoes
1 T butter
Salt and pepper

1 onion, sliced
1 cup sweet cream
1 t paprika

Scald potatoes and drain. Saute onion in butter until tender. Add cream and onion to potatoes, season, sprinkle top with paprika and bake in 350° oven for 1 hour.

POTATOES AND EGGS
Kartofle z Jajami

3 boiled potatoes
6 hard-cooked eggs
3 T butter

1 cup sour cream
Salt and pepper

Slice potatoes. In a buttered casserole arrange a layer of potatoes, a layer of sliced eggs and top with potatoes. Cover each layer with butter, seasoning and sour cream. Bake 30 minutes at 350°. Use 1 potato and 3 eggs to each layer.

POTATO CROQUETTES
Pączki Kartoflane

4 or 5 medium sized potatoes,
  boiled
1 T butter
4 egg yolks
3 T sour cream

1 onion, grated
2 T butter
3 T flour (heaping)
Salt and pepper

Mash hot potatoes, add melted butter. Beat egg yolks with sour cream and add to potatoes. Brown onion in butter and add to potatoes. Add flour and seasoning. Beat thoroughly. It should look like soft yeast dough. Fold in beaten egg whites. Drop by spoonfuls into butter or deep fat and fry to delicate brown.

96

FEATHER DUMPLINGS
Pulchne Kluseczki z Kartofli

2 medium sized boiled
  potatoes
3 eggs, well beaten
1 cup flour

1 t salt
Small cubes fried bread
Slice of onion

Rice the boiled potatoes. Beat eggs well. Combine with flour, salt and potatoes. Fry small cubes of bread brown in butter with a slice of onion. Shape potato mixture around bread cubes into small balls. Drop into slowly boiling salted water. Cover tightly and let cook for 15 minutes. Do not lift cover before that time as the dumplings will fall and be heavy.

POTATO PANCAKES
Placki z Kartofli

2 cups grated raw potatoes
2 T flour
2 well beaten eggs

1 t salt
1 t sugar

Pour off dark water accumulated on top of grated potatoes. Add the ingredients and beat well. With spoon drop mixture on hot griddle and spread as thinly as possible. Fry on both sides.

POTATO CAKES
Racuszki z Kartofli

3 cups cold mashed potatoes
1 T chopped onion
2/3 cup milk

4 slices bacon, crisp and
  chopped
Salt and pepper

Combine the ingredients. Drop from spoon on hot griddle and shape into cakes. Fry on both sides to a golden brown.

POTATO SALAD
Sałata z Kartofli

6 large potatoes
1/2 cup mayonnaise
1 apple
2 stalks celery, cut fine
1 dill pickle, chopped fine

1 T parsley, minced
1 T fresh dill, chopped
1/2 cup sour cream
3 T vinegar
1 t salt

Cook potatoes in boiling salted water until tender. Peel and dice. While still warm, add mayonnaise and allow to chill thoroughly in refrigerator. To the chilled potatoes, add peeled and diced apple and remaining ingredients. Chill before serving.

97

BEET SALAD
Sałata z Buraczków

4 medium sized beets, cooked
½ cup walnuts
Juice of ½ lemon
½ t salt

1 T sugar
1 T minced parsley
1 green onion, chopped

Slice beets very thin. Grind walnuts fine. Combine ingredients and toss lightly with a fork.

CABBAGE SALAD
Sałata z Kapusty

1 small head cabbage
Juice of ½ lemon
1 t salt
1 grated apple

½ t dill seed
Dash of grated garlic
1 T powdered sugar
½ cup salad oil

Shred cabbage fine. Mix with salt and lemon juice. Let stand four hours. Prepare dressing with grated apple and remaining ingredients. Add to cabbage and toss lightly.

SAUERKRAUT
Kapusta Kwaszona

5 lbs. sound and mature
   cabbage

2 ozs. salt
Caraway seed, optional

Remove outside green and dirty leaves. Cut head in half and take out core. Shred the cabbage finely and put five pounds of cabbage and two ounces of salt into a large vessel and mix with the hands. Pack gently into a crock with potato masher. Repeat until the crock is nearly full. Cover with a cloth, plate and weight. Fermentation will be complete in 10 to 12 days. During the curing process, kraut requires daily attention. Remove the scum as it forms and wash and scald the cloth often to keep it free from scum and mold. One pound of cabbage will fill one pint glass jar.

As soon as kraut is thoroughly cured, pack into glass jars, adding enough weak brine made by dissolving two tablespoons salt to a quart of water, to fill jars to within ½ inch of top. Put on cap, process in water bath for 15 minutes.

Or you may prefer not to cure the cabbage in a crock for 10 to 12 days but pack directly into jars. Follow the directions and mix well with the hands. Then pack solidly into clean glass jars. Fill with cold water. Put on cap, screwing band firmly tight. This will ferment for 3 to 4 days and will be ready for use in four to six weeks. One of the principal causes of failure

98

in making sauerkraut is the use of too much salt. Proper amount is 2½% by weight of the cabbage packed.

Use of caraway seed is optional. A ¼ teaspoonful through a quart jar or thin sprinkling through the bulk cabbage in crock improves its flavor.

SAUERKRAUT WITH WHOLE DRIED PEAS
Groch z Kapustą

1 qt. sauerkraut	1 cup whole dried peas
½ cup mushrooms, chopped	Salt and pepper

Wash peas and soak in water over night. Cook in same water, and add more if you have to, until tender, about one hour. Rinse sauerkraut. Wash and chop mushrooms. Cover sauerkraut and mushrooms with water, add salt and cook for one hour. Add peas, put into buttered covered baking dish and bake for half hour at 325°. Smelts or anchovies are sometimes added to this dish for **Wilia** supper.

If you decide to serve sauerkraut and peas on days other than fast days, cook sauerkraut and peas in the same way. When sauerkraut and peas are tender, thicken with a sauce made as follows:

½ lb. salt pork or bacon, chopped	2 T flour
1 onion, chopped fine	1 cup sauerkraut liquid

Fry onion with salt pork or bacon, until lightly browned. Blend in flour and add liquid. Stir until smooth and mix with sauerkraut and peas.

DILL PICKLES IN OPEN JAR
Letnie Ogórki Kwaszone

½ bushel firm cucumbers	3 cups sugar
Dill	10 qts. water
1 lb. salt	Grape leaves

Line bottom of stoneware jar with grape leaves. Cover with a layer of dill. Fill with washed cucumbers to within three inches from top. Cover with a layer of dill. Mix water with salt and sugar and cover cucumbers. Fermentation will be completed from 10 days to 2 weeks. After active fermentation has stopped, dill pickles must be protected against spoilage, as the brine is not sufficiently strong to preserve them long. One method is to seal in glass jars, another is to cover the pickles in the stoneware jar with melted paraffin.

DILL PICKLES
Ogórki Kwaszone

½ bushel firm cucumbers
Brine
Dill
Garlic (optional)

16 cups water
1 cup vinegar
¾ cup salt

Make brine of 1 cup of salt and 3 gallons of water. Soak cucumbers in brine over night. Drain and wipe dry. Fill quart jars with cucumbers, a sprig of dill and half bud of garlic. Boil the 16 cups of water, vinegar and salt; pour boiling hot over the cucumbers. Seal immediately.

If you can get soft well water for making brine, omit the vinegar. Vinegar helps to overcome the alkalinity of chemicals used to purify city water.

DILL PICKLES
Kwaszone Ogórki

½ bushel firm cucumbers
3 gallons ice water
1 cup salt
For each quart:
Sprig of dill
1 slice onion

½ bud garlic
1 ring green pepper
1 t horseradish
1 ring red pepper (optional)
Pinch of alum

Add salt to water. Wash cucumbers and soak in water over night. Drain, wipe dry. Pack into quart jars. Add rest of ingredients.

Cover with brine made as follows:

20 cups water
1 cup salt

2 cups vinegar

Boil the solution, skim and pour hot into the jars. Seal at once.

100

HARVEST FESTIVAL
DOŻYNKI

When the harvests are gathered the people of the fields give thanks and celebrate in an age-old custom called **Dożynki.**

On a warm Sunday in late August the tillers of the soil with their whole families walked gayly to the manor house to the music of the fiddle and the bass viol.

Heading the procession were pretty young maids in their colorful native costumes. They carried large wreaths made of the harvested rye, of wheat, intertwined with poppies and bachelor buttons. The fruit of the orchard—plums, pears and apples—was tied to the wreaths with yellow, red, blue and purple ribbons.

At the manor house the **Pan** greeted his people with bread and honey served on a large wooden platter. He invited the guests to his home where they sat down to long tables laden generously with various roasted meats, with coffee-cakes, poppy-seed breads, **babki,** and a good supply of wine, **wodka** and honey.

Good wishes were exchanged and everyone joined in the folk songs. They sang of love and work, they even sang of tragedies and funny things. Their hard work was over and their hearts were light and happy.

After the hours of feasting there were games for children, and dances. What a gay array of color, of spark and high spirit when the young people in their bright beaded and richly embroidered costumes swung into their **Krakowiak, Kujawiak, Mazur, Obertas,** while the older folk watched, or some, forgetting their tired bones, joined the dancers with a **hop sa dana, dana!** The celebration often lasted to daybreak.

To the people of the land the **Dożynki** to this day is a festival symbolic of the joy and gratitude for fair weather, for good crops —for the bounty of nature to mankind.

101

MUSHROOMS
GRZYBY

Mushrooms have a variety of uses. They make delicious main-course dishes. They are also used for flavoring meat, fish and vegetables, for soups, for sauces—all in all, mushrooms are a very useful as well as a delicious food. They contain many elements of nutritive value and are rich in mineral salts.

No doubt they are as old as man. The Pharaohs of ancient Egypt knew and prized them as a food and believed they grew mysteriously, magically, over-night. In Greek mythology they are the "food of gods." The Roman poets sang of these dainty vegetables. The art of cultivating mushrooms originated in France in the 17th century, when the other arts flourished. The fame of their flavor grew, and the new art spread to England. From there it was brought to America by English gardeners who grew their mushrooms in greenhouses. Although it is only fifty years since this art was introduced to America, we have so improved these methods that with modern canning and cultivation, American housewives are supplied with these morsels the year round.

There are many varieties of mushrooms in Poland, both the wild and cultivated. There are **borowiki, maślaki, bedłki, pieczarki, trufle, smardze, rydze** and others. If you have a relative or friend in Poland, ask him to send you a string of dried mushrooms. We refer to them often in the recipes. These grow wild and abundantly and are picked by the people. There is nothing like them for aroma and flavor. They are unusual and delicious. Before the war, Poland exported dry mushrooms to the United States.

Mushrooms in Poland are an important food. They are used as a dish for **Wigilia** Supper and often as a substitute for meat on fast days.

Mickiewicz, the great Polish poet, writes in his epic **Pan Tadeusz,** " . . . From the noisy breakfast they had gone out to the solemn ceremony of mushroom-gathering . . . Of mushrooms there were plenty; the lads gathered the fair-cheeked fox-mushrooms . . . for the worms do not eat them, and, marvelous to say, no insect alights on them; the young ladies hunted for the

102

slender pine-lover, . . . All were eager for the orange-agaric; this, though of more modest stature . . . is most delicious, whether fresh or salted, whether in autumn or in winter." And later, " . . . from the woods there came a throng carrying boxes, and baskets, and handkerchiefs with their ends tied up—all full of mushrooms . . . "

MUSHROOMS IN BUTTER
Grzyby w Maśle

1 lb. mushrooms	2 T buttered crumbs
3 T butter	1 t parsley, chopped
1 T onion, chopped	Salt and pepper

Fry onion in butter. Slice mushrooms and add to onion. Add seasonings and simmer slowly for one hour. When mushroom liquid disappears, add crumbs, mix well and serve hot.

CREAMED MUSHROOMS
Grzyby Duszone

1 lb. mushrooms	1 T flour
1 medium onion, chopped	1 cup sweet cream
3 T butter	Salt and pepper

Chop mushrooms. Cover with boiling water. Saute onion in butter. Strain mushrooms and add to onion. Season and cook for 30 minutes. Blend flour with cream, add to mushrooms and simmer for 10 minutes.

CREAMED MUSHROOMS
Grzyby Duszone

1 lb. mushrooms	1 T bread crumbs
1 large onion, chopped	1 cup sweet cream
3 T butter	Salt and pepper

Slice mushrooms. Saute onion in butter and add mushrooms. Cook until mushroom liquid disappears and only butter remains. Add bread crumbs. Last, add cream and simmer until thoroughly heated.

CREAMED MUSHROOMS
Grzyby w Sosie

1 lb. mushrooms	1 cup sweet cream
4 T butter	2 T sherry
2 T flour	Salt and pepper
½ cup chicken stock	

Slice mushrooms and saute in 2 tablespoons of butter for 10 minutes. Heat rest of butter, add flour and when smooth, add chicken stock and cream. Season. Bring to boiling point and simmer for 5 minutes. Add cooked mushrooms. Pour sherry into the mushroom frying pan to catch all the browned butter and add to other mixture. Serve on toast.

CREAMED MUSHROOMS
Grzyby Duszone

1 lb. mushrooms	1 T butter
2 T butter	1 T flour
2 T lemon juice	1/2 cup sweet cream
Salt and pepper	1 egg yolk

Slice or chop mushrooms. Fry in 2 tablespoons of butter with lemon juice until the mushroom liquid cooks away. Season. Heat butter, add flour. When blended, add to mushrooms with the sweet cream. Simmer slowly. Add beaten egg yolk, mix well and serve.

MUSHROOMS WITH SOUR CREAM
Grzybki z Kwaśną Śmietaną

1 lb. mushrooms	1/2 cup sweet cream
1 large onion	1/2 cup sour cream
Salt and pepper	Grated cheese
1 T flour	Butter

Cut onion fine and fry in butter until soft. Cut mushrooms into small pieces. Add to onion, season and fry until all liquid disappears. Add flour and mix well. Add sweet and sour cream and stir well. Remove to baking dish, sprinkle with grated cheese, pour melted butter over top. Place dish in shallow pan filled with water and bake until mixture becomes solid.

BAKED MUSHROOMS
Grzyby Pieczone

1 lb. mushrooms	2 eggs
Meat stock	Salt and pepper
1 hard roll	Dash of mace
Milk to moisten	1 t butter

Cook mushrooms in a small amount of meat stock. Season. Chop fine. Moisten hard roll with milk and squeeze dry. Add roll, eggs and seasonings to mushrooms. Mix well. Fill buttered patty shells or ramekins. Pour a teaspoon of melted butter over the tops. Set dishes in pan of water and bake for 15 to 20 minutes in moderate oven.

BROILED MUSHROOMS
Grzyby Pieczone

1 lb. large open mushrooms	Oil or butter
Salt and pepper	Juice of 1 lemon

Clean and remove stems. Season and rub with oil or butter. Broil for 10 minutes. Sprinkle with lemon juice. Excellent for garnish.

104

STUFFED MUSHROOMS
Grzyby Nadziewane

1 lb. large open mushrooms
Salt and pepper
Butter
Stuffing:

1 cup mushroom trimmings
1 onion, chopped
2 T bread crumbs
1 T chopped parsley

Remove stems from mushrooms. Wash, drain and season with salt and pepper. Spread a little butter over the caps and place in hot oven for 5 minutes. Chop mushroom stems. Lightly brown onion in butter and add chopped mushrooms. Season. Fry for 10 minutes. Thicken with bread crumbs and add parsley. Mix well and fill mushroom caps. Sprinkle with bread crumbs, spread a little melted butter over the top and brown in a hot oven or under broiler.

MUSHROOM CUTLETS
Kotlety z Grzyb

1 lb. fresh mushrooms or
1/4 lb. dry mushrooms
1 T butter
1 onion, chopped
6 hard rolls

1 T parsley, chopped
3 eggs
1 T bread crumbs
Salt and pepper

Chop mushrooms fine. Fry in butter with onion and parsley. Moisten hard rolls and squeeze dry. Add eggs and bread to mushrooms. Season to taste. Make small cutlets in the palm of your hand. Dip in bread crumbs and fry in butter. Mashed potatoes may be substituted for hard rolls.

MUSHROOM CUTLETS
Kotletki z Grzybów

10 large flat mushroom heads
1/2 t salt
1 egg

4 t flour
4 t butter
Bread crumbs

Wash mushrooms thoroughly in cold water. Dry carefully. Beat egg, add flour and salt. Dip mushrooms in egg mixture, then in bread crumbs and fry in butter until tender and brown.

MUSHROOMS WITH RICE
Grzyby z Ryżem

1 cup rice, wild or domestic
1 lb. mushrooms
3 T butter
Salt and pepper

1 cup sour cream
1/2 t beef extract
Chopped parsley

Slice mushroom caps and cook them in butter in a frying pan for about 10 minutes or until well browned. Add beef extract and sour cream. Heat but do not cook and taste for seasoning. Put a border of cooked rice around a platter and put the mushrooms in the center. Garnish with chopped parsley. Excellent tasting dish.

MUSHROOM SOUFFLE
Suflet Grzybowy

1 lb. mushrooms
1 T onion, chopped
6 T butter
6 T flour
Salt and pepper

2 cups scalded milk
½ cup grated cheese
6 eggs
½ cup chopped almonds

Cook and chop mushrooms and mix with chopped onion. Fry in butter under cover, allowing the mushrooms to steam and the flavors to blend. Make a white sauce of the butter, flour and milk. Add grated cheese. Beat egg yolks. Add ½ cup of white sauce to egg yolks to prevent curdling and mix with remainder of white sauce. Add mushrooms and almonds. Fold in stiffly beaten egg whites and bake in 325° oven from 50 to 60 minutes. Serve at once.

MUSHROOM OMELET
Omlet z Grzybkami

¼ lb. mushrooms
1 t chives, chopped
6 eggs
3 T butter

½ cup milk
Salt and pepper
Dash of paprika

Slice mushrooms. Saute in butter, add chives and seasoning. Mix the eggs lightly with a fork and add ½ teaspoon salt. Do not beat eggs stiffly thinking the omelet will be lighter. On the contrary, it will become heavier and watery. Add milk to eggs Heat a generous amount of butter in a heavy iron skillet and pour in the eggs. Bake in 400° oven for 20 minutes. Cut omelet in half, spread with mushrooms and cover with the other half. Serve immediately.

MUSHROOMS AND EGGS
Jajecznica z Grzybkami

½ lb. mushrooms
1 T chives or shallots
4 eggs

Salt and pepper
2 T butter
2 T sweet cream

Prepare mushrooms as above. Break eggs into a bowl and mix with fork and add seasoning. Melt 1 tablespoon butter in skillet and add the eggs, mixing with spoon. Let them cook over very

106

low heat, always stirring the eggs to keep them creamy and free from lumps. When they come to the point of forming a cream, gradually add the rest of the butter and the cream. Last add mushrooms, mix lightly and serve bordered with mashed potatoes.

CANNED MUSHROOMS
Marynowane Grzyby

1 peck mushrooms	½ cup salt
2 qts. water	2 large onions, quartered

Wash mushrooms thoroughly. Cover with water, salt, onions and cook for half hour. Fill hot jars, seal and boil in water for 30 minutes. To use, soak in cold water to remove salt and prepare according to any recipe for fresh mushrooms.

CANNED MUSHROOMS
Marynowane Grzyby

1 peck mushrooms   Salt

Wash mushrooms thoroughly. Arrange in layers in crock and sprinkle each layer with 1 tablespoon of salt. Weight down and let stand for 24 hours. Boil for half hour, pour into hot jars and seal.

EASY PICKLED MUSHROOMS
Łatwe Grzybki Marynowane

1 8-oz. can button mushrooms	1 bay leaf
1 cup mild vinegar	1 t pickling spices
2 T sugar	(in cloth bag)
1 t salt	

Bring vinegar and spices to boiling point. Add mushrooms and liquid and boil for 3 minutes. Cool. Serve whole on toothpicks for canapes or finely chopped, spread on plain or toasted rounds of white, rye or whole wheat bread or salted crackers and serve as appetizers.

PICKLED MUSHROOMS
Grzyby Marynowane

1 peck mushrooms	Small white onions
2 qts. vinegar	Whole pepper, allspice and
Olive oil	bay leaf
¼ cup salt	

Wash mushrooms in cold water. Cook with vinegar and salt for 20 minutes. Let stand over night. Next day, drain, wipe dry and arrange in jars. Blanch and peel onions and put a few in each jar. Cook vinegar with whole pepper, allspice and bay leaf. Cool and cover mushrooms. Add 1 tablespoon of olive oil to each jar.

107

PICKLED MUSHROOMS
Grzyby Marynowane

1 peck mushrooms
2 T salt
1 onion, sliced

2 parts vinegar
1 part water
1 t salt to quart jar

Clean and wash mushrooms in several waters. Cook for 1 hour in salted water. Drain, rinse in cold water, and cover with boiling water. Cook another hour. Drain thoroughly and fill quart jars, placing the sliced onion in layers between the mushrooms. Cover with 1 teaspoon of salt. Measure vinegar and water. Bring to a boil and fill jars. Seal tight.

PICKLED MUSHROOMS WITH VEGETABLES
Grzyby Marynowane z Jarzynkami

1 peck mushrooms
½ cup salt

2 qts. water
¼ cup salt

Wash mushrooms, rinse in several waters. Soak overnight in gallon of water with ½ cup of salt. Drain and rinse. Cover mushrooms with 2 quarts of water and ¼ cup salt. Simmer 1½ hours. Drain and rinse in cold water.

Vegetables:
8 carrots
1 cauliflower
1 lb. wax beans
2 sliced cucumbers

6 green tomatoes
Small bunch of celery
6 onions
1 green pepper

Cook carrots. Cook cauliflower and green pepper together. Cook wax beans. Cook celery and onions together. Do not overcook vegetables—they are firmer underdone.

Salt sparingly the green tomatoes, cucumber slices and sliced onion. Drain and rinse.

Make syrup of
2 qts. white vinegar

4 cups white sugar
2 cups brown sugar

Boil syrup for 4 minutes. Add to syrup ½ teaspoon whole mustard seed and 3 whole cloves for each quart of mushrooms and vegetables. Add mushrooms and boil for 10 minutes. Fill hot jars and seal.

DRYING OF MUSHROOMS
Suszenie Grzyb

Select firm medium size mushrooms. Clean them thoroughly but do not wash them. Spread them on a sheet and keep in the sunshine for 2 or 3 days. Turn them from time to time so that they may dry out evenly. After three days, thread them on long strings and hang up again in the sunshine or in a well-aired room. When they are thoroughly dried, keep them tightly covered.

108

COOKING DRY MUSHROOMS
Gotowanie Suszonych Grzyb

Wash the mushrooms carefully to remove dust and embedded grit. Soak in milk over night. Use like fresh mushrooms in any recipe.

MUSHROOM POWDER
Proszek Grzybowy

Dry mushrooms until they are very hard and will crumble. Pound them in a mortar to a fine powder. Sift through a fine sieve. Excellent in meat sauces, roasts and poultry.

Unless you hunger after the earth, you will not likely pick your mushrooms. In season you will get them fresh from your grocer and he will have them for you all year round in cans. They are ready to use just as they come from the can—no washing or peeling is necessary. Because they are already washed and cooked, they are equivalent to approximately double their weight in fresh mushrooms. An 8 ounce can is equal to a pound of fresh mushrooms, making them economical to use. For your convenience we list the sizes of packs of mushrooms.

PACKS OF MUSHROOMS
Cans and Cups

There are three packs of canned mushrooms—Buttons, Sliced, and Stems and Pieces. Each pack comes in 3 sizes for home use: 2-ounce, 4-ounce, and 8-ounce.

Comparative quantities in cans and cups are as follows:

Type of Pack	Size	Quantity in Cups
BUTTON	2 oz.	½ cup (⅓ cup mushrooms 4 to 5 tablespoons liquid)
	4 oz.	1 cup (⅔ cup mushrooms ⅓ cup liquid)
	8 oz.	2 cups (1⅓ cup mushrooms ⅔ cup liquid)
SLICED	2 oz.	½ cup (⅓ cup mushrooms about 3 tablespoons liquid)
	4 oz.	1 cup (¾ cup mushrooms ¼ cup liquid)
	8 oz.	2 cups (1⅔ cups mushrooms ⅓ cup liquid)

109

STEMS AND PIECES	2 oz.	½ cup (⅓ cup mushrooms about 3 tablespoons liquid)
	4 oz.	1 cup (¾ cup mushrooms ¼ cup liquid)
	8 oz.	2 cups (1⅔ cups mushrooms ⅓ cup liquid)

A WAYSIDE SHRINE

O, Chryste, you have hung
For centuries above this Plain,
In sorrow carved by one
Who felt your pain,
And bore your cross,
And knew your sorrow for his own!
Among the grain
That he had sown
His heart-blood flowered
Poppies red:
And then he knew
The thorns that pressed
Upon your head,
And carved your features as his own!

—Victoria Janda

Star Hunger, 1942

110

DAIRY DISHES
POTRAWY MLECZNE I MĄCZNE

STUFFED EGGS
Jaja Faszerowane

Eggs (two per person)   1 T chopped chives or shallots
2 T melted butter   Salt and pepper

Cook eggs until hard. Cool for easier handling. With very sharp knife cut eggs in half lengthwise. Remove egg from shell, being careful not to break the shell, and chop fine. Add melted butter, chives and season. Mix thoroughly and fill shells. Fry in butter for 10 minutes face down.

EGGS WITH BECHAMEL SAUCE
Jaja z Sosem Beszamelowym

Hard-cooked eggs   Bread crumbs
1 uncooked egg   Butter
Bechamel Sauce (page 77)

Cool eggs and remove shells. Beat uncooked egg slightly. Dip eggs in egg, then in bread crumbs and fry in butter. Place on serving dish and cover with Bechamel Sauce.

BACON EGG CAKE
Grzybek ze Słoninką

1/4 lb. bacon   1/4 cup water
4 eggs   1/4 cup milk
Salt and pepper   1 T chopped chives or shallots
10 soda crackers   Slices of thin white bread
1 rounded T flour

Cut bacon in small pieces and fry until crisp. Break eggs into a bowl. Add seasoning, crushed soda crackers, flour, water and milk. Mix thoroughly with spoon. Pour over the hot fried bacon (leave all the bacon fat in the pan) and cook very slowly until almost done. Sprinkle chopped chives over top and cover with slices of bread. Let cook very slowly until the eggs are set. Cut in wedge shaped pieces and serve immediately. Excellent for breakfast or luncheon.

111

EGGS IN BULLS' EYES
Wołowe Oczy

6 eggs
6 slices Vienna bread

Butter
Cream

Remove centers from bread slices and saute crusts in butter. Cover bottom of baking pan with a thin layer of cream. Arrange bread crusts. Drop an egg into each crust. Season. Pour a teaspoon of cream on each egg and bake in 350° oven for 15 minutes. Garnish with lettuce and anchovies.

SCRAMBLED EGGS
Jajecznica

4 eggs
1 T cream
Salt

1 T butter
1 T onion or shallots, chopped

Saute onion in butter until transparent, not brown. Beat eggs with fork only enough to mix yolk with white and add cream. Pour into onion and butter and lift from bottom with spoon, keeping the eggs light and fluffy.

SCRAMBLED EGGS WITH HAM OR POLISH SAUSAGE
Jajecznica z Szynką lub Kiełbasą

4 eggs
1 T cream

½ lb. Polish sausage or
½ cup diced cooked ham

Fry sausage or ham until slightly brown. Remove part of the fat from frying pan. Mix eggs with cream and pour over sausage or ham. Fry slowly, mixing lightly with spoon. Serve with chopped parsley.

EGGS WITH HAM
Grzybek z Szynką

4 eggs
1 large onion or shallots

¼ lb. cooked ham, chopped
Salt and pepper

Chop onion very fine. Beat eggs slightly, add onion and ham. Season. Drop with spoon into butter or bacon drippings like small pancakes. Fry on both sides.

BACON FRY
Grzybek ze Słoninką

½ lb. diced bacon
2 cups flour
1 T salt
3 t baking powder

3 eggs, beaten
1 cup milk and water
2 T sugar

Fry bacon in heavy skillet until crisp. Leave a sprinkling of bacon in the skillet and pour over it one-half the batter made of other ingredients. Spread to sides of pan. When mixture is set, turn and spread on the browned side another layer of batter. Sprinkle with more bacon and drippings. Turn as soon as bottom of first layer is browned. Repeat layer of batter dotted with bacon and drippings until pan is full. Takes a strong, steady hand to turn the cake each time. Can be done. Turn cake out on large plate and serve cut in wedges. This dish, when made right with the brown lines showing all around, is fit for a king. Sounds complicated but really is not.

SAUSAGE PUDDING
Budyń z Kiełbasek

1 doz. small pork sausages
2 eggs
1 cup milk

1 cup flour
½ t salt
1 T chopped chives

Fry sausages until crisp and brown. Drain off most of the fat. Beat eggs for 2 minutes. Add flour, salt and milk. Mix until smooth. Add chives. Pour batter over sausages in frying pan. Bake in 450° oven for 15 minutes, then in 350° oven for 10 minutes. Turn out on platter. Serve piping hot.

EGG NOODLES WITH POPPY SEED
Kluski z Makiem

Egg noodles
½ cup milk

½ cup poppy seed, ground
3 T sugar or 2 T honey

Cook egg noodles in salted water. Strain but do not rinse with cold water. Scald milk, add poppy seed and sugar or honey and cook for 5 minutes. Add poppy seed mixture to the noodles. Serve hot.

EGG NOODLES WITH HAM
Makaron z Szynką

3 cups egg noodles, cooked
½ cup chopped ham

1 T ham drippings
Bread crumbs

Butter a baking dish and dust with bread crumbs. Mix noodles with ham and drippings and fill baking dish. Sprinkle top with bread crumbs. Bake in 350° oven for 30 minutes.

EGG NOODLE PUDDING
Makaron z Rodzenkami

4 cups flour
2 eggs
2 T water
2 T melted butter
3 T sugar

2 egg yolks
10 chopped almonds
½ cup raisins
1 t lemon rind, finely chopped

Make noodles from the first three ingredients. Cut into your favorite shapes and sizes. Cook in salted water, rinse with cold water and drain. Mix noodles with remaining ingredients. Fill a buttered baking dish dusted with bread crumbs and bake 1 hour at 275°. Serve with hard or fruit sauce. (Page 81).

113

RICE CAKES
Placuszki z Ryżu

3 cups cold rice, well cooked   ½ cup milk
3 T flour   1 t salt
2 eggs

Cook the rice the day before, otherwise the batter will stick to the frying pan. Add eggs to the rice, then mix in the flour, one tablespoon at a time. Add salt and milk. Pour small pancakes on the pan and fry medium brown.

PIEROGI

2 eggs   2 cups flour
½ cup water   ½ t salt

Mound flour on kneading board and make hole in center. Drop eggs into hole and cut into flour with knife. Add salt and water and knead until firm. Let rest for 10 minutes covered with a warm bowl. Divide dough in halves and roll thin. Cut circles with large biscuit cutter. Place a small spoonful of filling a little to one side on each round of dough. Moisten edge with water, fold over and press edges together firmly. Be sure they are well sealed to prevent the filling from running out. Drop **pierogi** into salted boiling water. Cook gently for 3 to 5 minutes. Lift out of water carefully with perforated spoon.

The dough has a tendency to dry while you are working. A dry dough will not seal completely. We suggest rolling out a large circle of dough, placing small mounds of filling far enough apart to allow for cutting, and folding the dough over the mounds of filling. Then cut with small biscuit cutter and seal firmly.

Never crowd or pile **pierogi.** The uncooked will stick and the cooked will lose shape and lightness.

Varieties of fillings:

Cheese

1 cup cottage cheese   3 T sugar
1 t melted butter   3 T currants
1 egg beaten   ¼ t cinnamon

Cream cheese with melted butter. Add other ingredients and mix well. Fill **pierogi.** Serve with melted butter and sour cream.

Krowa co dużo ryczy, mało mleka daje.

A noisy cow gives little milk: Great talkers are little doers.

Cheese

1 cup dry cottage cheese	1 T sugar
Dash of salt	1 egg
1 t lemon juice	1 egg yolk

Force cottage cheese through sieve. Mix with other ingredients thoroughly.

Cabbage and Mushrooms

1 small head cabbage	1 small onion, chopped fine
2 cups mushrooms	Butter
2 T sour cream	Salt and pepper

Quarter cabbage and cook in salted water for 15 minutes. Drain, cool and chop fine. Saute onion in butter, add chopped mushrooms and fry 5 minutes. Add chopped cabbage and continue to fry until the flavors blend. Add sour cream and cool.

Sauerkraut

Two cups sauerkraut may be substituted for the cabbage. Rinse and chop sauerkraut. Proceed as above.

Mushrooms

1 cup chopped mushrooms	2 egg yolks
1 onion, chopped fine	Butter
Salt and pepper	

Saute onion in butter. Add mushrooms. Season. Remove from fire, add egg yolks and stir well. Cool and fill **pierogi.** Serve with chopped onion browned in butter.

Mushrooms and Meat

½ cup cooked beef	Butter
½ cup chopped mushrooms	Salt and pepper
1 onion, chopped fine	2 T sour cream

Run cooked meat through meat grinder. Fry onion in butter until transparent, add mushrooms and meat. Season to taste. Add sour cream and cool before using.

Prunes

1 cup cooked prunes	1 t sugar
1 t lemon juice	

Soak prunes over night. Cook with sugar and lemon juice. When cool, remove stones and fill **pierogi.** Serve with bread crumbs browned in melted butter.

Ripe Plums

Plums	Cinnamon
Sugar	

Peel and stone plums. Fill cavity with sugar and cinnamon. Dip in sugar. Cover with dough and seal edges with egg white. Serve with whipped cream.

Fresh Berries

Blueberries   Cherries
Sugar

Sugar fruit generously for half hour before using.

Cooked Fruits

The fruit preserves or conserve must be thick.

Apples

6 apples   ¼ t cinnamon
½ cup sugar

Peel and put apples through coarse blade of grinder. Mix with sugar and cinnamon. Cover the cooked **pierogi** with thick sour cream, buttered bread crumbs, sugar and cinnamon. Bake in oven at 350° for 15 minutes.

EASY PIEROGI
Leniwe Pierogi

2 cups dry cottage cheese   ½ t salt
1 T butter   1 t sugar
4 eggs, separated   ½ cup flour

Force cheese through sieve. Rub thoroughly until free from lumps. Add butter, egg yolks, salt, sugar and flour. Beat thoroughly until light. Add well beaten egg whites and fold in carefully. Turn out on floured bread. Roll with hands into long narrow roll. Flatten and cut slantwise into pieces 2 inches long. Cook in salted boiling water until they rise to top. Lift with straining spoon and cover with lightly browned buttered crumbs. They are delicious with sour cream flavored with cinnamon and sugar.

Following is a more economical recipe for them:

1½ cups dry cottage cheese   1 egg
1 cup cooked mashed potatoes   ¾ cup flour
    Make as above.

Another variation:

2 cups dry cottage cheese   2 T sugar
1 cup fine dry bread crumbs   4 eggs
2 T butter   ¼ t salt
¼ cup currants

Force cheese through sieve. Add rest of ingredients and mix thoroughly. Form into little balls, roll in flour and cook in salted boiling water. They will take somewhat longer to cook than those without bread crumbs. Serve with melted butter or sour cream.

116

PLUM PIEROGI
Pierogi ze Śliwkami

4 cups raw potatoes, grated 2 cups flour
2 eggs 1 t salt
Whole blue plums

Pour brown water off potatoes. Add eggs, flour, salt and mix thoroughly. Make a narrow long roll on floured board. Cut into 1 inch pieces and into the center of each press a large whole plum. Pull up edges of dough and seal. Drop into salted boiling water to cook for 8 to 10 minutes, until they come to the surface. Serve with sauce made of heaping tablespoon of butter, ½ cup sweet cream, ¼ cup sugar and ½ teaspoon cinnamon. Heat this sauce. Open the dumplings with two forks, pour sauce over them.

You may substitute 4 cups of mashed cooked potatoes and add 1 tablespoon milk. These may be filled with chopped meat or chopped fish and fried in butter or deep fat.

YEAST DOUGH FOR PIEROGI
Pierogi na Drożdżach z Różnemi Farszami

2 cups flour 2 egg whites, beaten
1 cup lukewarm milk ½ cup butter
2 yeast cakes 1 T sugar
4 egg yolks 1 t salt
1 T sugar 2 cups flour

Scald milk and cool to lukewarm. Break yeast into milk. Add to flour, beat well and set aside to rise. Beat eggs with a tablespoon of sugar. Add to beaten yolks, butter, sugar and salt. Beat thoroughly. Fold in egg whites. Add 2 cups of flour and beat with spoon until the dough no longer sticks to the spoon. Let rise again. Cut pieces of brown paper 5 x 3 inches. Rub paper with butter and stretch a tablespoon of dough on each. Fill with your favorite filling, fold paper so that filling is enclosed and let rise. Bake for half hour in 350° oven. Remove paper, arrange on platter and serve with melted butter or any of the other **pierogi** garnishes, depending on the filling.

ENGLISH PIEROGI
Pierogi Angielskie

2 cups flour ¼ lb. beef marrow or butter
1 cup sweet cream 1 small glass wine
1 yeast cake 1 T sugar
4 egg yolks

Break yeast into cream. Add other ingredients and knead to a firm dough. Roll thin, cut into rounds and fill with marmalade, conserve, apples, gooseberries, cherries or plums. Fold over and seal edges. Fry in butter.

117

PASZTECIKI

2 cups flour
½ lb. butter

2 T sour cream

Cut butter into flour, bind with sour cream. Gather dough into ball and roll on floured board. Take 2 tablespoons cold butter and cut into very small bits. Scatter the bits over the rolled out dough and fold into three thicknesses. Roll out again and fold in 3, press down and wrap the dough in wax paper. Store in refrigerator for two hours or longer until ready to bake. Roll pastry just once this time to desired thickness and use immediately. Use following for filling:

1 lb. ground beef
1 large onion, chopped
1 t flour

2 hard cooked eggs
Salt and pepper
½ cup water

Brown beef in butter. Saute onion to a golden brown. Chop eggs and mix lightly. Season. Stir flour into drippings left from browning beef. Add water to make thin brown gravy. Pour over meat and cool it thoroughly. Put small mounds of filling on rounds of pastry, seal edges with milk and bake in 450° oven for 20 minutes. Serve them on toothpicks with Martinis sometime. You will like them.

LAZANKI WITH CHEESE
Łazanki z Serem

2 cups flour
1 egg
2 T water
1 cup dry cottage cheese

2 egg yolks
3 T cream
1 T sugar

Make dough of flour, egg and water. Knead until firm and roll out on floured board. Cut into 1 inch strips. Cut strips slant-wise into half inch pieces. Cook like noodles in salted boiling water. Drain, bathe in cold water and strain. Force cheese through strainer. Add yolks, cream and sugar and beat hard. In a buttered baking dish arrange a layer of **lazanki** and a layer of the cheese mixture until used up. Sprinkle with buttered bread crumbs and bake in 350° oven for half hour.

118

CHEESE CAKES
Serniki czyli Małdrzyki

2 cups dry cottage cheese   ¼ cup sugar
2 eggs   ¼ cup raisins, optional
2 T cream   1 cup flour

Force cheese through sieve. Add eggs, cream and sugar and beat thoroughly. Add flour and raisins. Roll into balls in the palms of your hands. Flatten and with a thimble make depression in center. Fry in butter. Fill depression with cooked fruit, sprinkle with cinnamon and serve with sour cream.

NALESNIKI
Naleśniki

3 eggs   ½ cup milk   1 T sugar
3 T flour   ¼ t salt

Beat eggs well, then carefully add flour to avoid lumps. Add milk and salt.

Use olive oil or unsalted butter in frying pan. They burn quickly in salted butter. Some cooks prefer to use a piece of salt pork on end of fork for greasing frying pan. When pan is hot, pour in a small amount of batter, only enough to make a paper thin pancake. When medium brown do not turn over but remove from pan. Spread with **good cherry or strawberry** jam. Roll and dust lightly with **powdered sugar and serve warm** as a dessert. By tilting the hot frying pan in all directions, the batter will spread quickly. To assure tenderness the pancake should not be turned. This is a secret of fine **naleśniki.**

Naleśniki

3 eggs   ½ t salt
¾ cup milk   6 T flour
2 T sugar

Beat eggs without separating. Mix sugar, salt and flour well together and stir quickly into the eggs. Add milk and beat hard. Have ready one or more heavy 6 inch (diameter) frying pans, lightly buttered and well heated. Pour just enough batter into each to cover the bottom of the pan when it is tilted and swirled. Shake the **naleśniki** over the fire until they are slightly brown on the bottom and firm to the touch on top. Do not turn. Put them aside to cool. This may be done several hours before serving. This recipe makes 16 to 18 pancakes.

Naleśniki

4 egg yolks   2 cups flour
2 t sugar   2 cups milk
2 t melted butter   1 t salt
4 egg whites

Beat egg yolks, sugar and butter together until thick and

119

creamy. Sift flour and salt and add to first mixture, alternating with additions of milk. Beat until smooth. Fold in stiffly beaten egg whites. Fry very thin cakes on hot well-greased griddle.

YEAST NALESNIKI
Naleśniki na Drożdżach

4 cups flour	2 T sugar
2 egg yolks	2 yeast cakes
1 whole egg	1 T melted butter
2 cups milk	¼ t salt

Soften yeast in lukewarm milk and add to beaten eggs. Stir in remaining ingredients. Beat until blended. Cover and set in warm place to rise—until light, about 1½ hours. Do not stir, but lift carefully by tablespoon and fry slowly on a hot, well-greased griddle. This is a heavier pancake and must be turned.

NALESNIKI
Naleśniki Parzone

2 cups sweet cream	6 sugar cubes rubbed on rind
2 cups flour	of lemon
1 T butter	6 egg whites, beaten
6 egg yolks	

Scald the cream and add flour. Cook over low heat. Add butter, stir well and cook until thick. Remove from heat, cool and add egg yolks and sugar. Carefully fold in egg whites and fry as above. Turn carefully because they are very delicate cakes.

CAKE NALESNIKI
Naleśniki Biszkoptowe

10 egg yolks	2 cups flour
¼ cup sugar	10 egg whites, beaten
1 cup sweet cream	

Beat egg yolks with sugar until lemon colored. Add flour and cream alternately. Fold in stiffly beaten egg whites and fry cakes on well greased griddle. When done on one side, turn. Keep bowl with batter in cold water while frying.

Fillings for **Nalesniki:**   **Cream**

4 egg yolks	1 T flour
3 T sugar	1 cup sweet or sour cream
1 t vanilla	1 t grated lemon rind

Beat egg yolks in top of double boiler over heat. Add remaining ingredients and continue to beat until thick. Cool. Place a tablespoon of filling on a **nalesnik** and roll. Sprinkle with powdered sugar.

120

Apples

2 large tart apples	1/3 cup butter
1/2 t cinnamon	1/3 cup sugar
3 T sugar	1/3 cup bread crumbs

Cook apples with sugar and cinnamon. Cool. Fill **nalesniki** and roll up. Place in baking dish and brush with melted butter. Mix sugar with bread crumbs and butter and sprinkle over top. Bake in 350° oven for 20 minutes.

Fruits

Any thick cooked preserves. Roll the cakes, sprinkle with red wine and powdered sugar and bake in 350° oven for 20 minutes.

Butter

1/2 cup sweet butter	1/2 cup sugar
Grated rind of orange	Juice of 1 orange
1 jigger cognac	

Mix until creamy. Spread on cakes and fold in two. Pour a teaspoon of brandy on each cake and light. Serve while hot.

Honey

1/2 cup butter	2 t orange juice
1 t grated orange rind	1/2 t salt
1 t grated lemon rind	1/2 cup walnuts
1/2 cup honey	1 T curacao liqueur
1 t lemon juice	

Cream butter and work into it the remaining ingredients. Store in refrigerator until needed. Spread a generous amount of the honey-butter mixture in the center of each cooled cake and roll up neatly. Place in heat-proof dish. At serving time put them into a moderate oven for about 10 minutes, just long enough to heat the cakes and soften the butter mixture. Serve at once on warm plates.

SOUR MILK
Kwaśne Mleko

1 qt. pasteurized milk	1 cup or more sour cream

Mix sour cream with milk and set in warm place for 24 hours. Chill and serve.

Sour milk is a popular food in Poland. It is made of rich, unseparated milk and served with a sprinkling of sugar and cinnamon or with fried potatoes flavored with chopped bacon.

We have discovered that by adding sour cream to our bottled milk and letting it sour slowly, you get a very desirable consistency in the soured milk.

121

PASTRIES
CIASTA

Handling of yeast doughs, the combined process of mixing, kneading and baking, is a special kind of skill. For beginners we suggest taking a basic recipe and mastering it. Baking is one of the cookery skills that you do well only after you have acquired the "feel" of the dough. But once you get the "feel" and make really good breads, rolls and coffee cakes, much satisfaction will come to you. And what good things can be made!

In Poland, yeast is by far the most commonly used leavening agent. The people prefer the dark breads for their daily fare, but for holidays and special occasions they procure the finest wheat flour, add to it sugar and eggs, dried fruits and spices, and make the bread as fine as cake and a feast in itself.

The sweet breads are known as **placki** to distinguish them from bread, **chleb.** Under the broad term of **placki** come the special names for the coffee cakes. The shapes and the ingredients determine these.

The most popular is the **Baba,** a provincialism for woman. The cake is always baked in a fluted tube pan. It resembles the skirt of a woman. **Babka,** a word commonly used for grandmother, is the same cake but in a smaller size. **Babeczka** is the diminution of the word. Small rolls or cup cakes are called **babeczki.**

Dziad, a beggar, is the name of a cake baked on a spit, barbecue style. The spit revolves and the batter is poured on. The fire bakes some points of the cake faster than others. As a result bumps form and they remind the Polish cook of the gnarls or knots in the beggar's cane.

Przekładaniec is the name for a loaf filled with dried fruits or when it is used as a wrapper to enclose a fruited spicy mass, alternating layers of filling and dough. It is a filled coffee cake.

Strucla Makowa, Makowiec are the poppy seed cakes. The dough is padded to a sheet and spread with butter and a mixture of poppy seed.

Another kind of **Strucla** is the braided coffee cake. The dough is divided into four strips and braided into a loaf. The top is

122

brushed with egg yolk and sprinkled with whole poppy seed.

Then there is the **Kołacz,** taken from the word **Koło** –wheel. The dough is rolled into a sheet, buttered well, sugared and spiced, strewed with fruit fillings, peels and nut meats. It is then rolled like a jelly roll. The ends are brought together to form a ring. The diminution of the word is **Kołaczki** for small rolls filled with fruit and nuts.

Other names for small rolls are **bułeczki,** a small wheat bun. **Rogaliki,** diminution for **rogi,**—horns—butterhorns. **Łuky** is the word for crescents—crescent rolls. There are other names and each distinguished by its shape.

We cannot call to your attention too many times the need for bringing all ingredients to room temperature for best baking results, unless otherwise specifically stated. The flour should be sifted before measuring and should be of room temperature. Butter, unless recipe calls for melted butter, should be in a soft and pliable state, so that it can easily be measured and leveled. The yeast should be fresh. Yeast grows best at a temperature between 80° and 85°. A higher temperature kills yeast; lower temperature retards growth. Fresh and dry granular yeast requires 5 to 10 minutes for softening; while dry yeast cake requires 20 to 30 minutes.

There are two methods for mixing yeast breads. One is the lukewarm milk method. Butter is creamed with sugar, yeast and lukewarm milk is added, and then the remaining ingredients. The other method is the hot milk sponge. It is made by bringing milk to a boil, gradually adding a small amount of the flour to the hot milk and stirring until smooth; cooling and adding the yeast. This sponge is set aside to rise and then the remaining ingredients are added. The sponge method gives you a finer-textured and more moist result. After the addition of all ingredients, the rising action is faster than in the other method. We recommend it.

Flavoring is a matter of choice. Poland does not use artificial flavors nor commercial extracts. Grated lemon and orange rind, lemon juice, chopped orange and lemon rind, vanilla bean, mace, ground nutmeg and bitter almonds are at the disposal of the Polish cook. After much experimenting we find ground cardamon most distinctive in flavor. Flavor is important!

Our recipes direct you to beat egg yolks with salt. Adding salt to egg yolks intensifies the yellow color of the yolks in the pastry.

We have found rendered chicken and goose fat a very desirable shortening in yeast pastries. It makes the pastry light and moist. The poultry fats must be clean and without flavor. They will help to stretch the butter requirement.

123

EASTER BABA
Baba Wielkanocna

1 cup milk	1 t vanilla
3 cups flour	¼ t almond
¼ cup lukewarm milk	1 cup chopped almonds
2 yeast cakes	1 cup chopped citron, orange
½ cup plus 1 T sugar	and lemon peel
2 t salt	½ cup melted butter
15 egg yolks	Bread crumbs

Scald the milk. Slowly add three-quarters cup flour to hot milk and beat thoroughly. Cool. Dissolve yeast in quarter cup of milk and a tablespoon of sugar and add to cooled mixture. Beat well. Let rise until double in bulk. Add salt to eggs and beat until thick and lemon-colored. Add sugar and continue to beat. Add to sponge with flavoring and remaining flour. Knead for ten minutes. Add butter and continue kneading for ten more minutes or until dough leaves the fingers. Add almonds and citron peels and mix well. Let rise until double in bulk. Punch down and let rise again. Punch down and put into fluted tube pan. Butter the pan, press blanched almonds around sides and bottom. Sprinkle with fine bread crumbs. Fill with dough to cover one-third of the pan and let rise one hour. Bake 50 minutes at 350°. Decorate with white lucre. Sprinkle with colored sugar or baker's confetti.

~~~~~~

"NASZA JEJMOŚĆ" CZYLI "BABY WIELKANOCNE"

Hałas, tartas, rwetes, wrzawa, łoskot, łomot, jak w młocarni,
W izbie parno, ścisk, kurzawa, drzwi wciąż skrzypią u spiżarni,
Znoszą masła, jaja, sery, mąki, cukry i korzenie;
Jak jest w domu dziewek cztery, jedna się za drugą żeni.

Skrobią, myją, w piecach palą, wiercą, tłuką, szyją, wrzeszczą,
Ledwie domu nie rozwalą, aż w piekarni belki trzeszczą.
Wszystko kłębi się, jak w garnku, ledwie na głowach nie chodzą.
"Co to jest? . . . czy wir w jarmarku? . . ." Gdzie tam, to
    święta nadchodzą.

Jejmość to jak Marek w piekle, torem czcigodnej prababy,
Żwawo, ogniście, zaciekle, bije na Wielkanoc baby.
Bije placki, jajeczniki, torty, mazurki, kołacze;
Z tych powodów takie krzyki — dlatego jejmość tak gdacze.

Zostawmy więc gospodynie przy jej ważnem zatrudnieniu,
Przy mące, drożdżach, rozczynie, formach, jajach i korzeniu.
Niech grzmi, trąca, łaje, bredzi, wstrząsa piekieł fundamenta,
Jutro pójdzie do spowiedzi, da Bóg, że się upamięta.

                        Author Unknown,
                        Written in the 19th century.

124

LUCRE
Lukier

½ lb. sugar in cubes   ½ cup water

Cook until thick and forms thread when blown. Stir in **one** direction until a thick white mass appears. For flavor use lemon juice, maraschino juice, orange juice, rum, strong black coffee, barberry juice or pineapple juice.

BABA

4 cups flour   3 yeast cakes
1 cup milk   1 t salt
1 cup butter   1 t vanilla
1 cup sugar   ¼ t almond
15 egg yolks

Add salt to egg yolks and beat until lemon-colored. Add lukewarm milk and yeast. Add one-half of the flour, mix well and let stand until double in bulk. Add remaining flour, sugar, butter and flavoring. Knead thoroughly until dough leaves fingers. Let rise until double in bulk. Punch down and let rise again. Butter a tube mold, sprinkle with bread crumbs and fill with dough one-third full. Let rise about one hour and bake **40** minutes in 350° oven.

BABKA—PODOLIAN STYLE
Babka Podolska

½ cup sugar
1 t salt
½ cup butter
1¼ cups milk, scalded
2 yeast cakes
5 cups flour
4 eggs, beaten
1 T grated orange rind
1 T grated lemon rind
½ cup almonds, chopped
1 cup raisins

Scald milk, pour over sugar and butter. Cool. Dissolve yeast with a little of the warm mixture and add to remaining milk mixture. Add one-half of the flour and beat well. Add salt to eggs and beat until thick. Add to mixture and mix well. Add remaining ingredients. Knead for 15 minutes. Cover and let rise until double in bulk. Place in well-buttered tube pan, sprinkled with fine bread crumbs and bake 45 minutes in 350° oven.

BABKA

½ cup soft butter
½ cup sugar
4 egg yolks
1 cup milk, scalded
1 cake yeast
Grated rind of 1 lemon
¼ cup lukewarm water

4 cups flour
1 t salt
½ t cinnamon
1 cup white raisins
1 egg yolk, beaten
2 T water
¼ cup chopped almonds

Mix butter and sugar in large mixing bowl. Add salt to egg yolks and beat until thick. Add to sugar and butter mixture. Add yeast softened in ¼ cup lukewarm water. Add lemon rind and cinnamon. Add flour alternately with milk and beat well to make smooth batter. Add raisins and knead with your hand until batter leaves the fingers. Let rise in warm place until double in bulk (about 1½ hours). Punch down and let rise again until double in bulk. Butter fluted tube pan generously, sprinkle with fine bread crumbs, and fill with dough. Brush with mixture made by beating 1 egg yolk with 2 T water. Sprinkle with almonds, let rise and bake 30 minutes in 350° oven.

HOLIDAY STRUCEL
Strucle Świąteczne

8 cups flour
2 cups milk
4 yeast cakes
8 egg yolks
2 cups sugar

1 t grated orange rind
1 t grated lemon rind
1 cup melted butter
4 egg whites, beaten
1 t salt

Dissolve yeast cakes in ½ cup of the milk. Make thin sponge by mixing yeast with rest of milk and 1 cup of flour. Mix thoroughly, sprinkle top lightly with flour and set aside to rise. Add salt to egg yolks, beat until thick and lemon-colored. Add sugar, rinds and mix with sponge. Add two cups of flour, alternating with the milk, and knead for half hour. Add remaining flour and butter and continue to knead until the dough comes away from the hand. Carefully fold in the beaten egg whites and knead lightly. Set in warm place to rise until double in bulk. Separate dough into 4 parts, roll into long strips and braid into loaf. Brush top with lightly beaten egg yolk and sprinkle with poppy seed. Let rise. Bake in 375° oven for 40 minutes.

Jak sobie kto pościele, tak się wyśpi.
As one makes his bed, so he must lie in it.

PRIZE-WINNING RECIPE FOR SMALL BABKA
Babeczka

3/4 cup hot milk
2 cups flour
1 yeast cake
1 T warm water
2 T soft butter
1/3 cup sugar

1/2 t salt
2 egg yolks
1/2 t cardamon, ground
Raisins, chopped nuts,
    chopped cherries, optional

Scald milk. Carefully stir 1/2 cup flour into hot milk. When smooth and cool, add yeast softened in warm water with 1 teaspoon sugar. Set aside to rise. Add salt to egg yolks and beat until thick. Add to sponge the butter, sugar, beaten egg yolks and cardamon. Beat with spoon thoroughly. Slowly add the remaining 1 1/2 cups of flour and knead with hand until dough no longer sticks to the fingers. Let rise until double in bulk. Punch down and let rise again, about one hour. Bake in loaf, tube or sheet pan to suit your fancy, for 30 minutes in 350° oven.

BABA AU RHUM
Babka z Rumem

2/3 cup lukewarm milk
3 yeast cakes
3 cups flour
1/2 t salt
12 whole eggs

1/2 t cardamon
1 lemon rind, grated
1 cup butter
1/2 cup sugar

Dissolve yeast in milk with 1 teaspoon sugar and 2/3 cup flour. Beat until well blended and let rise in warm place for 15 minutes. Add salt to eggs and beat until thick. Cream butter, add remaining sugar gradually. Add beaten eggs and lemon rind. Add remaining flour and beat for 10 minutes with electric mixer. Cover, let rise until double in bulk, about one hour. Punch down, let rise again until double in bulk. Butter tube pan generosly, dust with fine bread crumbs. Pour in batter, let rise in warm place for half hour. Bake in 350° oven for 50 minutes. Remove from pan and pour Rum Sauce over top and sides.

RUM SAUCE
Sos z Rumen

1/2 cup sugar
3/4 cup apricot juice or
1/2 cup water

1 t lemon juice
1/2 cup rum

Cook sugar with fruit juice or water for five minutes. Add lemon juice and pour over top and sides of **babka.** Spoon the rum over this. Serve warm with whipped cream.

BABA AU RHUM
Babka z Rumem

½ cup milk
1 yeast cake
¼ cup sugar
½ t salt
2¼ cups flour

2 T soft butter
4 egg yolks
½ lemon rind, grated
6 ozs. candied cherries

Scald milk and cool to lukewarm. Crumble yeast into milk and stir until dissolved. Add salt to egg yolks and beat until thick. Add sugar, salt and 1 cup of flour to milk and yeast and beat until smooth. Add beaten egg yolks. Add remaining flour, lemon rind and chopped cherries and beat with spoon until spoon becomes free of dough. Set in refrigerator and chill for at least 12 hours. Punch down and let rise until double in bulk. Turn into a well-buttered crumb-lined 9 inch tube pan and let rise until triple in bulk. Bake in 350° oven for 30 minutes. See recipe for Rum Sauce above.

BABA AU RHUM
Babka z Rumem

½ cup milk, scalded
1 yeast cake
2 cups flour
½ cup sugar
½ cup butter

3 eggs
½ t salt
¼ t mace
1 lemon rind, grated

Dissolve yeast in cooled milk. Mix with 1 tablespoon of sugar and ½ cup flour. Beat until well blended. Let rise in warm place until double in bulk, about half hour. Cream butter and sugar, add eggs beaten with salt, lemon rind, mace and remaining flour. Add yeast mixture and beat well, about 10 minutes with electric mixer. Butter tube pan, sprinkle with bread crumbs. Pour in batter and let rise until triple in bulk, about 1½ hours. Bake 40 minutes in 350° oven. Remove from pan and pour Rum Sauce over top and sides.

POPPY SEED COFFEE CAKE
Strucla z Makiem

1 yeast cake
1 T warm water
½ cup scalded milk
2 T butter
¼ cup sugar

½ t salt
2 egg yolks
2 cups flour
¼ t ground cardamon

Cream butter with sugar. Add salt to egg yolks and beat until thick. Scald milk and cool to lukewarm. Add beaten yolks

128

to butter and sugar mixture. Add yeast dissolved in 1 tablespoon of warm water. Add flavoring and mix thoroughly. Add flour alternately with the milk and knead with hand until fingers are free of dough. Let rise for about 2 hours or until double in bulk. Punch down and let rise again for one hour. Place dough on floured board and roll to one-half inch thickness into rectangular shape. Spread with poppy seed mixture and roll like jelly roll, sealing all edges. Place in baking pan and let rise until double in bulk. Bake for 45 minutes in 350° oven.

POPPY SEED FILLING

1 cup ground poppy seed
¾ cup milk
½ cup sugar or ⅓ cup honey

1 egg
1 t vanilla

Bring milk to boiling point and add poppy seed. Cook for about 5 minutes, stirring carefully, until milk is absorbed. Add sugar or honey. Beat egg thoroughly. Mix 1 tablespoon of hot poppy seed with egg and pour into cooked poppy seed. Stir until thick. Add vanilla. Must be thoroughly cooled before using.

APPLE COFFEE CAKE
Przekładaniec Jabłkowy

5 cups sifted flour
1 cup sugar
1 cup milk
3 whole eggs
½ cup butter
2 yeast cakes
1 t vanilla

1 t almond
1 t mace
1 t salt
4 medium sized apples
½ cup sugar
1 t cinnamon, optional

Dissolve yeast in one-half cup lukewarm milk. Add one teaspoon of sugar and let stand for 10 minutes. Heat the other half cup milk only warm enough to melt butter and sugar. Cool to lukewarm. Add salt to eggs, beat well and add to butter mixture. Add 4 cups of flour and beat thoroughly with spoon. Let stand until double in bulk, about one hour. Work down with spoon. Add remaining cup of flour and beat thoroughly. Let rise until double in bulk. Spread on well floured board and roll to one-half inch thickness. Cover with peeled and sliced apples,

129

half cup sugar and cinnamon, if you like. Roll like jelly roll and seal edges. Butter an 8x12 pan, sprinkle with bread crumbs and fill with coffee cake. Let rise for one-half hour. Bake one hour in 350° oven. Remove from oven and top with lucre or butter icing while warm.

FILLED COFFEE CAKES
Przekładańce

5 cups flour	½ t ground cardamon
5 T sugar	1¼ cup milk
1 t salt	½ cup chopped nut meats
2 yeast cakes	½ cup seedless raisins
½ cup butter	1 t cinnamon
3 egg yolks	5 T sugar

Sift flour, sugar and salt. Crumble yeast over the dry ingredients. Work the butter in as for pie crust. Add well beaten egg yolks and milk, mix well and let rise for 2 hours. Punch down and let rise again. Spread on well-floured board and roll half inch thick. Sprinkle with chopped nut meats, raisins, cinnamon and sugar. Roll and seal edges. Let rise 2 hours before putting in 375° oven for one hour.

FILLINGS FOR COFFEE CAKES
Mixed Filling

1½ lbs. ground poppy seed	½ cup chopped raisins
1 cup honey	¼ cup butter
3 cups thin cream	1½ cups walnuts, ground
1 cup sugar	

Mix ingredients in large iron skillet. Place over a low fire, stirring constantly until thick, for about 30 minutes. This burns easily. Cool before spreading on dough. This is enough to spread about one-quarter inch thick.

Nut Meat Filling

1 lb. mixed nut meats, chopped	1 cup sugar
½ cup butter	1 lemon rind, grated
1 egg	Cinnamon or vanilla
	¼ cup cream

Melt butter, add beaten egg. Brush dough with butter and egg mixture. Spread with chopped nut meats. Cover with sugar, lemon rind, cinnamon and cream.

Walnut Filling

2 cups ground walnuts	½ cup milk
½ cup butter	2 egg yolks
1 cup sugar	

Mix ingredients and cook for 5 minutes. Cool and spread on dough.

130

Cottage Cheese Filling

1 lb. dry cottage cheese	½ cup sugar
4 egg yolks	Grated lemon rind
1 T melted butter	½ t vanilla
½ cup raisins	

Press cheese through strainer. Mix with egg yolks, butter, sugar, lemon rind, vanilla and raisins. Spread on dough.

Raisin Filling

¼ cup seedless raisins	1 cup milk
½ t grated lemon rind	

Mix ingredients and cook until thick.

Prune Filling

2 cups cooked chopped prunes	¼ cup brandy
	½ cup sugar
1 cup chopped nut meats	¼ t nutmeg

Mix ingredients, cover and let stand over night.

Date Filling

1 cup chopped dates	2 T lemon juice
1 cup chopped nuts	¼ t mace

Mix ingredients thoroughly and spread on dough.

Almond Filling

1 cup almond paste or	⅞ cup powdered sugar
¼ lb. ground almonds	1 egg white
½ t almond extract	

Grind almonds (if almond paste is not used), add sugar gradually and stir until smooth. Mix with egg white and spread on dough.

PRUNE TART
Placek z Suszonych Śliwek

1 yeast cake	2 egg yolks
1 T sugar	½ cup sugar
½ cup milk	3 T melted butter
1 cup flour	1¼ cups flour
½ t salt	Cinnamon
Thick sweet cream	Sugar

Soak prunes in warm water over night. Scald milk and cool to lukewarm. Dissolve in it the yeast cake and the tablespoon of sugar. Add 1 cup flour and allow to rise in warm place until warm and spongy. Add eggs, sugar and butter, remaining flour and salt. Knead slightly and let rise until double its bulk. Roll dough to half inch thickness and put in oblong pan with sides at least one and one-half inches deep. Pull dough to the top of the sides and allow to rise for half hour. Brush with melted butter and pour in thick sweet cream to a depth of from three-quarters to a full inch. Pit the prunes and lay them in close rows on the dough and sprinkle heavily with cinnamon and sugar. Bake in 350° oven for half hour. Serve warm or cold.

FRUIT ROLLS
Nadziewane Ciastka

4 cups flour	1 cup sugar
1 cup milk, scalded	1 cup melted butter
3 yeast cakes	1 t grated lemon rind
8 egg yolks	½ t ground mace
1 t salt	

Dissolve yeast cakes in ½ cup of the milk. Milk must be lukewarm. Make sponge of yeast and milk and 1 cup of flour. Mix thoroughly and set aside to rise. Add salt to egg yolks, beat until thick and lemon-colored. Add sugar, flavoring and mix with sponge. Add two cups of flour, alternately with the milk and beat with electric mixer for 20 minutes. Add remaining flour and butter and continue to knead with the hand until the dough comes away from the sides of the bowl. Set in warm place to rise until double in bulk. Punch down and let rise again. Spread on floured board and roll to one-half inch thickness. Make the rectangle not more than 10 inches wide. Spread filling to half inch thickness and roll like jelly roll. Cut slantwise in one-inch pieces. Let rise until double in size. Bake 25 minutes at 350°.

Filling

1½ lbs. dry bread crumbs	2 t vanilla
1½ lbs. white raisins	3 cups sugar
¾ lb. butter	½ t salt
½ lb. chopped almonds	cream to moisten

Sift the dry bread crumbs. Puff raisins in hot water and drain. Mix bread crumbs, raisins, butter, sugar and cream and cook over a low fire. Add salt and flavoring. Cool thoroughly.

BABA CAKES WITH APRICOTS
Babeczki z Morelami

1 yeast cake	2 egg yolks
1 T warm water	½ t salt
½ cup milk, scalded	½ cup sugar
1½ cups flour	1 T orange rind, chopped fine
⅓ cup soft butter	

Cream butter with sugar. Add yeast dissolved in warm water. Add egg yolks beaten with salt and orange rind. Cool milk and add alternately with the flour. Beat for 10 minutes with electric beater. Let rise until double in bulk. Butter individual muffin tins, sprinkle with fine bread crumbs and half fill with dough. Let rise and bake in 350° oven for 25 minutes. Remove a small piece from top of each cake. Insert a cooked apricot or a teaspoon of apricot marmalade, replace the top and serve immediately with sherry sauce.

132

SHERRY SAUCE
Sos z Winem

½ cup butter
1 cup sifted powdered sugar

2 or 3 T Sherry Wine

Beat butter until smooth and creamy. Add powdered sugar gradually. Add the sherry slowly and beat until smooth.

COTTAGE CHEESE ROLLS
Kołaczki Ze Serem

1 cup milk, scalded
¼ cup butter
½ cup sugar
1 t salt
2 eggs
4½ cups flour

1 yeast cake
¼ cup warm water
1 t grated lemon rind
1 t grated orange rind
1 t vanilla

Pour milk over butter and sugar; stir until dissolved. Cool to lukewarm. Dissolve yeast in warm water and add to milk mixture. Add salt to eggs, beat well and add to milk mixture.

 Add rinds and flavoring. Add half the flour and beat until smooth. Add remaining flour, mix thoroughly and knead for about 10 minutes. Cover and set in warm place to rise about 1 hour. Punch down, brush with melted butter, cover and store in refrigerator overnight. Roll out on floured board to one-fourth inch thickness and cut into small squares. On each square, place a little of the cottage cheese filling and pinch the four ends of the square over the filling crosswise to form four eyes. Place on greased cookie sheet and brush with beaten egg yolk. Let rise until double in bulk. Bake in 350° oven for half hour.

Cottage Cheese Filling

1 lb. dry cottage cheese
2 eggs, separated
½ cup sugar
2 T butter
1 T flour

1 T lemon juice
1 T lemon rind
½ t salt
½ t vanilla

Press cheese through sieve; add egg yolks, sugar, butter, flour, lemon juice and rind, salt and vanilla. Mix well. Beat egg whites stiff and fold in carefully.

133

KOLACHKY*
Kołaczki

1 cup potato water
1 cup hot milk
2 yeast cakes
1 cup flour
2 eggs or 4 yolks

6 cups flour
1 cup sugar
2 T salt
½ cup melted butter

Heat milk to boiling point, add to cold potato water. Crush 2 yeast cakes into this liquid, add 1 cup flour, beat until smooth and let rise one-half hour. Add remaining flour, sugar, salt and butter and knead very thoroughly until dough forms soft ball. Cover and let rise until double its bulk, about 2 hours. Roll out on floured board until dough is one inch thick. Cut into 2 inch squares. Fill squares with fruit filling (prunes, dates, apricots or cottage cheese). Pinch corners of squares together, being certain fruit is completely enclosed in square. Place in buttered pans and let rise one hour. Brush tops with melted butter and bake in moderate oven, 350°, for 45 minutes or until nice and brown.

Variation: 1 cup of raisins may be added to dough while kneading and dough may be spread out on pan into coffee cake. Sprinkle top with brown sugar, butter and cinnamon.

*Submitted by a member with Slovak background.

COTTAGE CHEESE CAKE
Serowiec

8 large graham crackers
1 T sugar

⅓ cup melted butter
¼ t cinnamon

Roll graham crackers fine. Mix with other ingredients and press firmly into the sides and bottom of an 8 x 11 inch cake pan. Keep 2 tablespoons of crumbs to sprinkle over top of cake.

Cheese Filling

1 lb. dry cottage cheese
4 eggs
1 cup sugar
½ t salt
¼ cup flour

½ t vanilla
1 cup heavy cream
Juice of 1 lemon
Grated rind of 1 lemon

Press cheese through sieve. Add salt to eggs and beat thoroughly. Add sugar, flavoring and cream. Carefully fold in the cheese and flour. Mix well. Pour on graham cracker crumbs in pan. Sprinkle remaining crumbs on top. Bake 1 hour in 250° oven. At end of hour, turn off heat and leave the cake in oven for another hour. For a large cake double or triple the recipe.

134

CREAM CHEESE CAKE
Serowiec

18 pieces zwieback   1½ T sugar
1½ T butter

Crush zwieback fine, mix with butter and sugar and line bottom of spring form mold.

4 packages Philadelphia   1 cup sour cream
   cream cheese   1 inch length vanilla bean
1 cup plus 2 T sugar   4 egg yolks
2 T flour   4 egg whites
¼ t salt

Cream the cheese to a fluff. Add sugar, flour, salt and vanilla and beat. Add the beaten yolks. Mix well and add the sour cream. Fold in the stiffly beaten whites, pour into crumb lined pan and bake in 350° oven for about one hour.

COTTAGE CHEESE CAKE
Serowiec

3 lbs. dry cottage cheese   1 t vanilla
3 cups sugar   1 lb. graham crackers
½ cup flour   1 t cinnamon
1 t salt   ½ cup sugar
1 cup rich cream   2 T melted butter
12 medium eggs

Force cheese through colander. Sift sugar with flour and salt, add to cheese and mix. Beat egg yolks and add to cheese mixture. Add cream and flavoring, mix. Beat egg whites until stiff but not dry and fold into mixture. Roll graham crackers fine, add cinnamon, ½ cup sugar and melted butter. Save one-half cup of the crumbs for the top of the cake. Butter tube pan generously, line with the cracker crumb mixture. Pour in cheese mixture. Sprinkle with the half cup crumb mixture, bake in 350° oven for 1½ hours. 60 servings.

COTTAGE CHEESE CAKE
Serowiec

2 cups flour   ½ t salt
¼ lb. butter   Grated rind of 1 lemon
6 T sugar   3 T cream
4 egg yolks

Beat butter with sugar to a white mass. Add yolks beaten with salt, lemon rind and flour. Mix with hand thoroughly. Spread

---

Nie będzie z tej maki chleba.
There will be no bread from that flour:That cannot succeed.

on baking pan to half-inch thickness and bake for 30 minutes at 350°.

While it is baking, prepare the following cheese topping:

2 lbs. dry cottage cheese	3 egg whites, beaten
1/4 lb. butter	1 T flour
8 egg yolks	1/2 cup sugar
2 T lemon juice or	Grated nutmeg
1 t vanilla	

Press cheese through sieve. Add butter, egg yolks and sugar. Beat thoroughly. Mix flour carefully and add flavoring. Fold in the beaten egg whites. Spread on cake, sprinkle top lightly with grated nutmeg. Return to oven for 30 minutes at 325°.

PĄCZKI

1 1/2 cups milk	1 t vanilla
2 yeast cakes	1/2 t mace or
1 t salt	1/2 t nutmeg
1/2 cup sugar	1/2 cup butter
3 egg yolks	4 1/2 cups flour
1 whole egg	

Scald milk and allow to cool to lukewarm. Break yeast into lukewarm milk. Beat sugar and butter until fluffy, add eggs, salt and flavoring. Add flour and milk gradually, beating well. Let rise in warm place until double in bulk. (About 2 1/2 hours). Punch down, knead and let rise again. Place dough on lightly floured board, stretch toward you and fill with thick filling (jelly is not thick enough). Fold over and cut into desired size ball, place on lightly floured surface and let rise. Fry in deep hot fat, turning only once. Pączki should have a very dark color before turning to insure that they are thoroughly baked. Drain on soft absorbent paper. Sprinkle with vanilla-flavored powdered sugar or a mixture of granulated sugar and cinnamon.

Frying Hints: The temperature of the fat can be tested by dropping in a cube of bread, about one inch in size. If it browns in one minute, the fat is hot enough. This is a good general rule to remember when frying any uncooked food. Be sure, above all, that the fat does not smoke. Add a tablespoon of cold water to the cold fat to keep it from burning easily and to insure a nice browning of the food. Fat may be used over and over again, if clarified after each use and stored properly. To clarify, let the fat cool, add a few slices of raw potato, and heat slowly until the potato is well browned. Strain through several thicknesses of cheesecloth. Store in a tightly closed container in a cool, dark place. When re-using, fry a quartered apple in the fat to remove any flavor.

136

EXCELLENT WARSAW PĄCZKI
Wyborne Warszawskie Pączki

1 cup sweet cream	5 T soft butter
2 yeast cakes	4 cups flour
10 egg yolks	1 jigger rum
1 t salt	6 T sugar

Heat cream to lukewarm. Add salt to egg yolks and beat until thick. Cream butter and sugar. Put these ingredients into a large bowl, add yeast dissolved with 1 tablespoon of sugar and mix thoroughly. Add rum, then flour and cream alternately and beat hard until the dough blisters. Set in warm place to rise. Punch down and let rise again. Proceed to fill and fry as above.

PĄCZKI

6 cups flour	1½ cups milk
3 yeast cakes	1 cup less 2 T melted butter
20 egg yolks	1 cup sugar
1 t salt	1 jigger rum

Scald milk. Carefully add 1 cup of flour to the hot milk, stirring until smooth. When cool, crumble yeast into the mixture and mix thoroughly. Let rise for half hour. Add salt to egg yolks and beat until thick and lemon-colored. Add eggs, sugar and rum to the sponge and mix. Add remaining flour and knead until dough no longer sticks to the hand. Last add butter and knead until thoroughly blended. Let rise until double in bulk. Punch down and let rise again. Proceed to fill and fry as above.

This recipe will make about 20 **pączki**. An excellent Polish cook uses as many egg yolks as she makes **pączki**.

PĄCZKI

4 cups warm flour	1 orange rind, grated
3 whole eggs and 6 yolks	½ cup cream, ½ cup milk
½ cup butter, melted	¾ cup sugar
2 yeast cakes	1 t salt

Beat eggs with sugar. Add cool melted butter and beat thoroughly. Add orange rind, salt, warm cream and milk. Beat well. Add warm flour gradually and continue to beat. Add yeast dissolved in 1 tablespoon warm milk and mix thoroughly. Beat dough about ten minutes and set aside to rise. When double in bulk, punch down, and let rise again. Proceed to fill and fry as above.

CHRUST

4 egg yolks	1 t vanilla
1 egg white	1 T rum
¼ cup powdered sugar	1 cup flour
½ t salt	

Add salt to eggs and beat for 10 minutes. Add sugar and

137

flavoring and beat until well blended. Fold in the flour. Transfer to a well-floured board and knead until the dough blisters. Cut in halves, roll very thin and cut into strips about 4 inches long. Slit each piece in center and pull one end through the slit. Fry in hot fat until lightly browned. Drain on absorbent paper and sprinkle with powdered sugar.

CHRUST

5 egg yolks
½ t salt
3 T sugar

5 T sour cream
2½ cups flour
1 T brandy or cognac

Add salt to eggs and beat until thick and lemon-colored. Add sugar and flavoring and continue to beat. Add sour cream and flour alternately, mixing well after each addition. Knead on floured board until the dough blisters. Proceed to cut and fry as above.

CHRUŚCIK

2 cups flour
2 whole eggs
4 egg yolks
½ t salt

½ cup powdered sugar
¼ cup butter
1 jigger rum

Add salt to eggs and beat until thick and lemon-colored. Add sugar, butter and rum and continue to beat. Fold in flour and knead until the dough blisters. Proceed to cut and fry as above.

FAVORITES
Faworki

2 whole eggs
2 egg yolks
½ t salt
4 T sugar

1 t cream
1 t butter
1 cup flour
½ t almond extract

Beat eggs with salt. Add sugar, cream, butter and flavoring. Add flour, mix well and turn out on floured board. Knead until smooth and firm. Proceed to cut and fry as **"chrust."**

STRUDEL

1½ cups flour
¼ t salt
1 egg
⅓ cup warm water
2 qts. sliced tart apples

1 cup seedless raisins
1 t cinnamon
½ cup melted butter
1 cup sugar

Sift flour and salt together. Place in large mixing bowl and blend in the unbeaten egg. Add the warm water and mix the dough quickly with a knife. Knead it on a well-floured board,

stretching it up and down to make it elastic and until it leaves the board clean. This is absolutely necessary to develop the elasticity of the flour gluten to the point where it will stretch without breaking.

Toss it on a well-floured board and cover it with a warm bowl. Keep it warm for a half hour or longer. Lay the dough in the center of a well-floured tablecloth on a large table. Brush well with melted butter. Then with hand under dough, palm down, pull and stretch the dough gently, and then gradually around the edges until it is as large as the table and thin as paper. Sprinkle the apples, raisins, sugar and cinnamon evenly over three quarters of the dough. Drip over all a few tablespoons of melted butter. Trim the edges.

Then fold the dough over the apples on one side. Now hold cloth high in both hands and the strudel will roll itself over and over into a big roll. Trim off the edges again. Then twist the roll to fit a large greased pan. Bake in hot oven 425° until brown and crisp. Brush with melted butter.

CHERRY COBBLER
Placek z Czereśni

Weigh 3 eggs	Flour, the weight of 3 eggs
Butter, the weight of 3 eggs	3 egg yolks
Powdered sugar, the weight	3 egg whites
of 3 eggs	Sweet cherries, pitted

Cream butter to a froth. Add powdered sugar and egg yolks and beat hard. Add the flour and fold in carefully the stiffly beaten egg whites. Spread on buttered pan and cover with pitted sweet cherries. Bake 25 minutes at 350°. Sprinkle top with powdered sugar and serve warm or cold.

Three average eggs weigh 5 ounces. Three large eggs weigh 7 ounces.

APPLE TEA CAKE
Torcik Jabłkowy

3 cups flour	3 eggs
1 cup butter	½ cup sugar

Cut butter into flour with knife like shortening in pie crust. Add eggs and sugar and mix thoroughly. Roll out and line baking pan. Bake in moderate oven for 25 minutes.

139

2 lbs. apples   Sugar—weight of peeled and cored apples
Cover apples with sugar, add no water, and simmer until they become transparent. Cool and cover the cake. Decorate with almond halves and candied fruits.

APPLE CAKE
Jabłka na Kruchym Cieście

1 cup butter	1 t vanilla
3 cups flour	½ t salt
1 cup sugar	6 apples, pared and sliced
2 egg yolks	½ t cinnamon
2 T sour cream	1 cup sugar

Sift flour, sugar and salt. With knife cut butter into the flour mixture until crumbly. Add egg yolks, vanilla and sour cream and mix thoroughly. Spread on buttered cookie sheet. Cover with apples mixed with sugar and cinnamon. Bake for 30 minutes in 350° oven.

UPSIDE DOWN CAKE
Szarlotka Owocowa

3 eggs	½ t vanilla
¼ t salt	2 T boiling water
1 cup sugar	1 cup cake flour

Beat eggs with salt until thick and lemon-colored. Add sugar gradually and beat. Add vanilla and water. Fold in the flour. In bottom of buttered pan arrange thick cooked fruit or apple sauce. Pour batter over fruit and bake for 30 minutes in 350° oven.

ROYAL MAZUREK
Mazurek Królewski

1 cup butter	¼ cup almonds, chopped fine
6 egg yolks	1½ cups flour
1 cup sugar	¼ t salt

Cream butter. Sift flour, sugar and salt. Add alternately one egg yolk and a little flour until all has been used. Add almonds. Bake in a 17 x 11 pan for 30 minutes at 350°

CHOCOLATE MAZUREK
Mazurek Czekoladowy

1 cup sugar	1 t vanilla
4 egg yolks	1 cup dry bread crumbs
4 ozs. baking chocolate	4 egg whites, beaten
4 t butter	

Cream sugar and butter. Add beaten egg yolks. Add chocolate, vanilla and bread crumbs. Fold in egg whites. Mix

140

well and spread one-half inch thickness on buttered and bread crumb dusted pan. Bake at 350° for 15 minutes. Turn off the heat and leave in oven for 10 minutes.

MAZUREK

½ cup butter	2 cups flour
1 cup sugar	1 egg
3 T cream	¼ t salt

Sift the dry ingredients. Cut butter into flour with knife until crumbly. Mix beaten egg with cream and add to flour. Mix lightly with hand and spread on buttered cookie sheet. Bake for 20 minutes in 350° oven. Remove from oven and quickly cover with one of a variety of toppings. Bake 20 minutes longer. When cool decorate with lucre, maraschino cherries, angelica, chopped candied orange peel, cocoanut, etc. Cut into small 1 x 2 inch pieces. This is a rich and delicious pastry.

TOPPINGS FOR MAZUREK
Mixed Fruits

½ lb. raisins	Juice of 1 lemon
½ lb. dates	Juice of 1 orange
½ lb. figs	1 cup sugar
¼ lb. nut meats	2 eggs

Chop fruits and nuts. Do not put through food grinder. Add sugar, eggs and flavoring and mix well. Spread on baked pastry and return to oven for 20 minutes.

Citrus Fruits

4 oranges	½ cup water
1 lemon	1½ cups sugar

Remove seeds from fruit and grate the whole fruit. Bring sugar and water to boiling point. Add the grated fruit and cook carefully until it becomes thick. Remove from fire, stir until cool. Cover the pastry baked for 30 minutes in 350° oven. Set in cold place to cool.

Apples

2 cups sugar	12 sliced apples
1 cup water	Grated rind of lemon

Boil sugar and water to thick syrup. Add apple slices and boil slowly until glossy. Add grated rind. Cool and spread on partially baked pastry. Return pastry to oven for 20 minutes.

Dates

6 egg whites	½ lb. dates sliced lengthwise
1 lb. powdered sugar	½ lb. grated baking chocolate
½ lb. chopped almonds	

Beat egg whites until stiff and slowly add the sugar. Beat for half hour. Add other ingredients, mix well and spread on baked pastry. Return to oven for 20 minutes.

141

Lemon

1 cup sugar   ½ lb. chopped almonds
1 egg   Juice and rind of 1 lemon

Beat sugar, egg and flavoring until thick. Add almonds and spread on baked pastry. Return to oven for 10 minutes.

Chocolate

12 cooked egg yolks   ½ lb. almonds, chopped
8 ozs. baking chocolate 1 egg
2 cups sugar   1 t vanilla

Rub cooked yolks through sieve. Beat egg with sugar. Add melted chocolate and egg yolks. Add vanilla and chopped almonds and spread on baked pastry.

WALNUT TORTE
Tort Orzechowy

12 eggs, separated   6 T flour
1 cup sugar   ½ lb. walnuts, ground fine

Beat egg yolks until thick and lemon-colored. Add sugar gradually. Add the walnuts and flour and mix thoroughly. Fold in stiffly beaten egg whites. Bake in three well buttered 8 inch layer cake pans for 30 to 35 minutes in 350° oven.

Filling

½ lb. walnuts, ground fine   ½ cup sweet cream
1 cup powdered sugar
Mix well and spread between layers of cake.

Frosting

1 egg yolk   3 T brandy
1 heaping T butter   Powdered sugar to thicken

Mix and spread on top and sides of cake.

CHOCOLATE TORTE
Tort Czekoladowy

6 eggs, separated   10 T flour
8 T sugar   1 T cocoa

Beat whites of eggs until stiff but not dry. Add yolks one at a time and continue beating. Add sugar by the spoonful. Fold in the flour sifted with cocoa. Bake in 300° oven for 40 minutes.

Frosting

½ lb. ground walnuts   3 egg yolks
½ cup sugar   1 T brandy
½ cup milk   ¼ lb. butter

Over a slow fire cook the walnuts, sugar and milk. At end of 10 minutes, add egg yolks and mix thoroughly. Cool and add brandy. Cream the butter, add the nut mixture and beat 15 minutes.

142

CHOCOLATE TORTE
Tort Czekoladowy

6 eggs
1 cup sugar
¾ cup flour

¼ t salt
2 squares grated chocolate
1½ t. vanilla

Beat egg yolks until very thick and lemon-colored. Gradually beat in the sugar. Sift flour and salt together; mix thoroughly but lightly with the chocolate. Add flour mixture to egg yolks and sugar, in about 4 portions. Beat well and add flavoring. Fold in egg whites, beaten stiff but not dry. Bake in a well-buttered spring form pan or deep, round layer cake pan at 325° for 30 minutes. Remove from pan and cool. Split cake in half, fill with sweetened whipped cream into which finely shaved or shredded Brazil nutmeats have been folded.

CHOCOLATE TORTE
Tort Czekoladowy

30 eggs, separated
1 lb. baking chocolate
2 lbs. sugar

1 t vanilla
¼ cup rye bread crumbs
¼ cup potato flour

Beat egg yolks until thick and lemon-colored. Add melted chocolate, sugar and vanilla, beat well. Sift bread crumbs fine and add. Beat egg whites until stiff. Fold into mixture. Blend in potato flour. Butter and dust pan with bread crumbs and pour in mixture. Bake in 325° oven for one hour.

ALMOND TORTE
Tort Migdałowy

6 eggs
1 cup sugar
¾ cup chopped almonds

1 T grated orange rind
⅓ cup cracker meal
Whipping cream

Beat 3 whole eggs and 3 yolks with the sugar, adding a little sugar at a time. Do not blanch the almonds but run them through the finest knife of your food chopper. Roll soda crackers and sift before measuring. Add the almonds and cracker meal alternately, then the orange rind. Beat remaining 3 egg whites stiff but not dry and fold into the mixture. Turn batter into 2 well buttered 8 inch layer cake pans and bake 45 minutes at 325°. When cooled on a cake rack, spread whipped cream flavored with a tablespoon of brandy and tablespoon confectioner's sugar between the layers and on top.

LEMON TORTE
Tort Cytrynowy

5 eggs
1 cup sugar
⅓ cup water
1 cup cake flour

½ t salt
2 T lemon juice
1 t lemon rind, grated

Beat whites until stiff but not dry. Boil sugar with water to soft ball stage and slowly add to beaten whites. Add salt, lemon juice and rind to egg yolks and beat until thick and lemon-colored. Combine with egg white mixture carefully. Fold in the flour. Pour into tube pan, set into cold oven, and bake 35 minutes at 350°.

PASTRY FINGERS
Paluszki

1 lb. butter
1 lb. dry cottage cheese

4 cups flour
½ t vanilla

Put cheese through grinder. Mix with soft butter and flour, first cutting in with knife, then lightly kneading. Make little balls the size of walnut and set in refrigerator over night. Roll each ball until very thin. Fill with any of the following mixtures: cottage cheese, dates, prunes, poppy seed or thick jam. Seal edges and make small rolls. Bake in 350° oven until light brown, about 15 minutes. Sprinkle with powdered sugar.

ALMOND PRUNES
Śliwki Migdałowe

2 lbs. large prunes
1 lb. blanched almonds
½ t salt

1 cup flour
2 eggs
⅓ cup milk

Soak prunes in warm water over night. Cook and cool. Remove stones, fill cavity with almonds, and let drain for few hours. Make batter of remaining ingredients. Dip prunes in batter and fry in deep fat. Roll in powdered sugar or granulated sugar mixed with nutmeg.

Variations of fillings: Raisins soaked in cherry brandy, also orange peel.

BABKI WITH CUSTARD FILLING
Babki Śmietankowe

2 cups butter
1 cup sugar
2 cups flour
2 eggs

Custard:
2 egg yolks
½ cup cream
½ cup sugar

Beat butter to a foam. Add sugar and eggs, beat well. Blend in flour. Cook egg yolks, cream and sugar in double boiler until thick. Butter cup cake tins and dust with bread crumbs. Line tins with dough, fill with cooked custard and cover with dough. Bake in 350° oven for 25 minutes.

144

BEGGAR'S CAKE
Dziad

2 lbs. butter
40 eggs
2 lbs. sugar

Grated rind of 10 lemons
2 lbs. potato flour
3 cups sweet cream

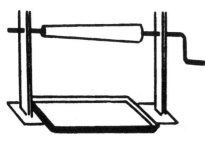

Beat butter to a pulp. Add one yolk at a time, alternating with a tablespoon of sugar until the mixture has been beaten for one hour. Beat the egg whites stiff and add by tablespoon, alternating with a tablespoon of flour. Add the grated lemon rind and finally the cream.

This cake is baked barbecue style. Get an oakwood rod the size of a rolling pin, about 16 inches high, wider at the bottom, narrow at the top. The rod should have a hole in it wide enough to make it fit on a spit. Wrap rod with well-buttered paper and tie securely with string. Support ends of rod with tripods. Place tray under rod for dripping batter. Bake before a blazing fireplace or a gas fire grate. Heat the rod to a high temperature. One person then turns the rod while another pours on batter with a soup

ladle. When first layer begins to brown, pour on another layer and so on until all the batter is used. The last layer should be baked most thoroughly. Add the batter from dripping tray. Cool cake for six hours on the rod. Cover the cake unevenly with lucre. Slice from the top.

Baking of this cake is not as difficult as it sounds. It is delicious and it keeps for a long time. In Poland 60 and 100 eggs are used in the recipe with other ingredients in proportion. This is a precious old recipe.

145

TEA CAKES
HERBATNIKI

CRISP BUTTER HORNS
Kruche Rogaliki

1½ cups flour
1 cup butter
½ cup almonds, chopped

⅔ cup sugar
1 t vanilla

Cream butter and sugar. Add almonds and vanilla. Blend in flour. Roll thin on lightly floured board. Cut into desired shapes. Bake in 375° oven for about 12 minutes. Remove from oven and dust with powdered sugar.

NEAPOLITAN CAKES
Ciastka Neapolitańskie

1¼ cups butter
1 whole egg
2 egg yolks
4 hard cooked eggs

4 cups flour
1 cup sugar
Rind of one lemon, grated
1 cup almonds, finely crushed

Cream butter and sugar, add uncooked eggs. Rub cooked eggs through sieve and add. Blend in flour, add lemon rind and almonds. Chill for one hour. Roll out and cut into desired shapes. Bake in 375° oven for 12 minutes.

GRYMASIKI

1½ cups sugar
1 t vanilla

1½ cups flour
3 whole eggs

Beat eggs, add sugar and vanilla. Blend in flour. Roll thin and cut into desired shapes. Bake in 350° oven for about 10 minutes.

BEZY

4 egg whites
2 cups powdered sugar

4 t lemon juice
1 t vanilla

Combine all ingredients and beat until very stiff. Drop by tablespoons on well buttered baking sheet. Bake in 300° oven for 30 minutes.

WAFERS
Sucharki Papieskie

⅔ cup butter
7 egg yolks
½ cup sugar

1 whole egg
2 cups flour
1 t baking soda

Cream butter, add alternately one egg yolk and one tablespoon sugar and beat well. Add the whole egg. Add flour and baking soda. Mix well. Put on floured board, roll to ¼ inch thickness and cut with round cookie cutter. Bake on well buttered baking sheet in 375° oven for 12 to 15 minutes.

146

HONEY COOKIES
Ciastka Miodowe

4 cups flour	¼ t ginger
½ cup honey	½ t cinnamon
1 egg	½ t nutmeg
2 egg yolks	¼ t cloves
½ cup sugar	Almond halves
1 t soda	

Combine sugar and honey. Add eggs and beat well. Sift flour with soda and spices, add to honey mixture. Mix well. Set in refrigerator to stiffen. Roll out to ¼ inch thickness on floured board and cut with round cookie cutter. Press half of one almond on top of each cookie, brush with egg white. Bake on buttered baking sheet in 375° oven for 15 minutes.

MAKAGIGI

1 lb. almonds, chopped	½ cup honey
⅔ cup butter	¼ cup sugar

Carmelize sugar, add honey, butter and simmer slowly for 20 minutes. Add almonds and cook 10 minutes. Line dish with waxed paper and drop by spoonfuls. Set in cold place to harden.

CHOCOLATE CAKES
Ciastka Czekoladowe

8 egg yolks	½ lb. milk chocolate
½ cup sugar	⅞ cup flour
1 cup almonds, chopped	

Melt chocolate. While it is melting, beat eggs and add sugar. Blend in chocolate. Add almonds and flour. Mix lightly. Mold with cookie press on buttered baking sheet. Bake 25 minutes in 325° oven.

RING COOKIES
Ciastka z Twardych Jaj

1 cup butter	Rind and juice of one lemon
5 egg yolks, hard cooked	1 cup sugar
3 whole eggs, uncooked	3 cups flour

Cream butter. Rub hard cooked egg yolks through sieve and add. Add remaining ingredients in order listed. Roll out on well floured board, or shape into small rings by rolling a teaspoon of dough to thickness of a pencil and shaping into a ring. Brush with egg white and sprinkle with sugar. Bake in 350° oven for 15 minutes.

FRUIT ROCKS
Ciastka z Bakaliami

1 cup butter
7 eggs
1 cup sugar
1 cup raisins
½ cup candied orange peel

½ cup almonds, chopped
½ cup milk or cream
1½ cups flour
1 t baking powder

Cream butter, add egg yolks one at a time. Beat. Add sugar and beat again. Add raisins, orange peel, almonds and the milk. Beat egg whites and add. Sift flour with baking powder and add to mixture. Mix lightly. Drop from teaspoon on buttered baking sheet. Bake in 325° oven for 20 minutes.

FRUITED PIERNIK
Piernik Wyborny

1½ cups honey
1 cup sugar
1 yeast cake
½ cup beer
1 T butter
4 cups flour
4 whole eggs
Pinch of pepper

½ t cloves
½ t cinnamon
½ t allspice
½ cup figs
½ cup walnuts
½ cup dates
2 T orange peel

Bring honey to boiling point. Add sugar and bring to boil twice. Cool. Dissolve yeast in warm beer, add to honey. Add butter, flour, eggs and beat well. Add remaining ingredients and mix thoroughly. Spread on buttered baking sheet. Bake in 350° oven for 40 minutes. Cut into desired pieces.

SMALL PIERNIK
Pierniczki Drobne

2 eggs
1 cup sugar
1 t vanilla
½ t almond

1 t baking soda
1 T water
1 cup honey, brówned
3 cups flour, white or rye

Beat eggs until lemon colored. Add sugar and flavoring. Add soda dissolved in water, honey, flour and mix well. Shape into tiny round balls or put on well floured board and shape into fingers or cut with round cookie cutter. Bake in 350° oven for 15 minutes. Frost if desired.

PIERNIK — HURRY! GUESTS ARE COMING!
Piernik Gwałtu! Goście Jadą

4½ cups flour
1 cup honey
1 cup sugar
2 eggs

2 t baking soda
1 T water
1 t vanilla
1 t salt

Beat eggs, add sugar, honey and flavoring. Dissolve soda in water and add. Sift flour and salt together and add to mixture. Mix well. Roll thin and cut with small cookie cutter. Brush with beaten egg yolk and sprinkle with sugar. Bake in 350° oven about 12 minutes.

MADELEINES
Magdalenki

8 egg yolks
1 cup sugar
1½ cups flour

½ cup butter
½ t salt
1 jigger rum

Beat eggs and sugar until lemon colored. Add flour and melted butter. Add rum. Fill buttered small cup cake tins about one-fourth full. Sprinkle with sugar and slivered almonds. Bake in 350° oven for 15 minutes.

POLISH TEA CAKES
Ciastka z Konserwą

½ cup butter
½ cup sugar
1 egg yolk, slightly beaten

1 cup flour
½ t salt
½ t vanilla

Cream butter and sugar until light. Add egg yolk, mix well. Add flour sifted with salt. Mix. Roll dough in small balls, dip in unbeaten egg whites and roll in finely chopped nuts. Place on buttered baking sheet and press down center of each with thimble. Bake in 325° oven for 5 minutes. Remove and press down again with thimble and return to oven for about 10 to 15 minutes. Remove from oven and fill indentation with preserves while still warm.

CINNAMON CUTS
Krajanki Cynamonowe

3 cups flour
3 whole eggs
1½ cups sugar
½ cup raisins
½ cup nut meats

1 t soda
1 T water
1 t cinnamon
1 T butter

Cream butter, sugar and eggs. Dissolve soda in water, add to mixture. Sift flour with cinnamon and add. Add raisins and nut meats and mix well. Roll into long strips about one inch thick and flatten to about two inches in width. Bake in 350° oven for 25 minutes. Remove from oven, slice diagonally and return to oven for 15 minutes. These will keep indefinitely.

149

DESSERTS
LEGUMINY

Choice of Polish desserts is determined by the time of the year and the heartiness of the meal. A light meal is ended with a heavier dessert; a heavy meal ends with a lighter dessert. Apple pie is unknown. Ice cream is served at very important parties.

In summer, desserts consist of fruits as they come into season. Every farm yard has its own orchard. After the first World War, **independent Poland decreed** that boulevards in the developing small towns be planted with cherry trees.

The fruit is served fresh with cheeses or cooked into compotes **and served cold.** Sometimes several fruits are combined. Fruit is a popular topping and filling for pastries. It forms the base of many gelatine desserts.

In winter, desserts are combinations of milk, eggs, cream with a thickening agent like farina, rice, bread or gelatin. Because these combinations are apt to be bland, the cook uses rum and wine for flavoring if she does not have fruit juices. Canned fruit is rare and rather expensive and the supply of home-dried and preserved fruit is dependent on the size of the summer's crop. Most of the desserts are substantial and served hot.

Often delicious pastries are served to end the meal. **Naleśniki** and **pierogi** in their limitless variations follow Lenten meals.

APPLE COMPOTE
Kompot z Jabłek

6 apples   2 cups water
1 cup sugar   Small glass of white wine

Peel, core and quarter apples. Boil water, add sugar and wine. Bring to boil again. Add apples and simmer slowly until tender. The quarters remain whole and become rich and golden with the addition of the wine.

APPLE COMPOTE
Kompot z Jabłek

5 apples   1 cup water
1/2 cup sugar   1/2 stick cinnamon or peel of
1 jigger white wine, optional   half lemon

Peel, core and cut apples in half. Bring sugar, water and wine to boiling point. Skim and add cinnamon or lemon peel. Add

150

apples and simmer only until tender. Lift out apples with straining spoon. Boil syrup to thicken it and pour over apples. Serve with a very thin sprinkling of finely chopped lemon peel.

BAKED APPLES WITH RED WINE
Jabłka na Winie Czerwonym

6 juicy apples	1 cup red wine
Cherry or strawberry preserves	½ cup sugar

Wash apples and remove cores. Do not bore through the apple but leave a half inch at bottom of apple. Fill with thick preserves. Place in baking dish and cover with wine and sugar. Cover and bake for one hour in 350° oven. Chill and serve.

JELLIED APPLE COMPOTE
Kompot z Jabłek w Galarecie

6 Winesap apples	2 T sugar
1 cup water	Peel of half lemon
1 jigger white wine	1 T gelatin
12 almonds, chopped fine	2 T cold water

Wash and peel apples but do not remove stems and do not core. Cover with water, wine, sugar, lemon peel and simmer until transparent. Cook carefully because they must remain whole. Arrange on serving dish and sprinkle with chopped almonds. Add one tablespoon of sugar to apple liquid, bring to boiling point and add gelatin dissolved in cold water. Mix thoroughly, cool and pour over apples. Chill and serve with whipping cream.

PEAR COMPOTE
Kompot z Gruszek

1 doz. firm pears	¼ t vanilla
2 cups white or red wine	3 whole cloves
1 cup sugar	

Peel pears, leaving stems attached. Bring to a boil the wine, sugar, vanilla and cloves. Add pears and simmer until pears are transparent and well colored. Remove pears and cook syrup down to the consistency of cream. Pour over pears. Serve ice cold with white cream cheese.

PEAR COMPOTE
Kompot z Gruszek

6 pears	2 cups water
12 whole cloves	¾ cup sugar
1 apple	1 jigger white wine

Peel, core and cut pears in half. Insert one whole clove in each piece of fruit. Bring water and sugar to boiling point and add quartered apple. Add wine and pears and simmer until pears are tender.

151

PEARS WITH RUM
Kompot z Gruszek z Arakiem

ô pears
2 cups water
¾ cup sugar
Rum, cognac or kirsch

½ cup currant jelly
1 t cornstarch
1 T cold water

Peel whole pears. Cook sugar and water to a light syrup. Add pears and cook until soft. Remove to serving dish. Cook syrup until reduced to about half of the original quantity and add currant jelly. Thicken with cornstarch mixed with water and pour over pears. Keep pears hot. Just before serving, heat rum, cognac or kirsch, pour over all and ignite at the table.

BERRY COMPOTE
Kompot z Malin lub Truskawek

1 lb. fruit, strawberries
  or raspberries

1 cup sugar
1 cup water

Wash fruit and drain thoroughly. Boil sugar and water to a syrup, skim and pour over fruit. Do not boil fruit in syrup but let stand for two hours before serving.

GOOSEBERRY COMPOTE
Kompot z Agrestu

1 lb. under-ripe gooseberries
1 cup sugar

1 cup water
1 inch stick cinnamon

Scald the clean berries with boiling water and strain. Make syrup of sugar, water and cinnamon stick. Add gooseberries, bring to a boil. Remove from fire and cool.

CHERRY COMPOTE
Kompot z Wisień

Cherries
Sugar

Vinegar

Remove pits from cherries, place in crock and cover with vinegar for 24 hours. Drain vinegar well and measure cherries. Add sugar cup for cup and mix well. Let cherries stand in a cool place for about two days, stirring frequently until sugar is dissolved. Put into jars and store. This compote will keep for a long time.

The drained vinegar may be used for usual purposes.

152

CHERRY COMPOTE
Kompot z Wisień

1 qt. pitted fresh Bing
  cherries
1 cup water
½ cup sugar

6 whole cloves
¼ cup lemon juice
¼ cup currant jelly

Combine cherries, water, sugar and cloves in a saucepan. Simmer gently for 15 minutes. Drain cherries and boil juice down to two cups. Add remaining ingredients to juice and boil to the jelly stage. Cool the syrup and pour over cherries. Chill in refrigerator for several hours and serve ice cold in sherbet glasses. Top with whipped cream. Eight servings.

BRANDIED CHERRIES
Konserwowane Wiśnie

1 can pitted black Bing
  cherries

½ cup brandy

Drain the juice from the cherries. Pour the brandy over them, let stand several hours. Drain again. Put them in chafing dish, light the flame under the dish, pour in some warmed brandy, turn the cherries over for a moment in the brandy, and pass the brandy spoon through the flame and into the dish. A burst of blue flame appears. Ladle the flaming cherries over and over until the brandy has almost burned out and put cherries and all over hard vanilla ice cream.

STRAWBERRIES IN PORT
Wyborny Kompot z Truskawek Na Winie

Strawberries
Sugar

Glass of port wine

Wash and hull berries. Drain well and put in glass serving bowl. Sprinkle with sugar and cover with a glass of port wine. Cover closely and chill for 1 hour. Do not let the berries stand too long as they soften rapidly under this treatment.

STRAWBERRIES IN RUM
Truskawki z Arakiem

3 lbs. strawberries   ½ pint rum
6 lbs. sugar

Hull and clean berries. Choose large select berries. Line a porcelain or earthen dish with a layer of berries, cover with sugar and spray with rum and let stand over night. The next day bring the berries to a quick boil on a hot fire, skim and let cool. Repeat this process of quick boiling three times. Cool and pour into sterilized jars. Will keep indefinitely.

BRANDIED PEACHES
Konserwowane Brzoskwinie

1 peck peaches, skinned   1 qt. brandy
Sugar to half their weight

Alternate in stone jar, layers of peaches with sugar until filled. Add brandy. Cover closely, using cheesecloth or unbleached muslin under the jar cover. Ready to use after one week. Keep in cool place.

BRANDIED PEACHES
Konserwowane Brzoskwinie

Peaches   Sugar to cover

Remove skins from peaches, put into quart jars. With sugar, fill up empty spaces and cover the peaches. Put jar lids on but do not screw them down tightly; omit jar rubbers. Inspect peaches every day and continue to add more sugar to cover peaches until juice is drawn from them and sugar is dissolved. When sugar has been dissolved and peaches are covered with juice, insert jar rubbers and put on cap, screwing band firmly tight. Wrap each jar in a good thickness of newspaper and store in a dark, dry place. In three months you will have delicious brandied peaches to serve with ice cream or pudding.

PEACHES IN RUM
Brzoskwinie w Araku

3 cups juicy, ripe peaches,   ½ cup honey
  sliced   Jigger of rum

Mix honey and rum together and pour over peaches. Chill thoroughly before serving. When ready to serve pour a little extra rum in another bowl and light it before it reaches the table. Ladle burning rum on cold fruit.

LEMON CREME
Krem Bardzo Łatwy

8 eggs, separated   1 T rum
7 T powdered sugar   1 T gelatin
Juice of large lemon   2 T cold water

Beat egg yolks with powdered sugar until thick. Add lemon juice and rum. Dissolve gelatin in cold water and steam over hot water until smooth. Add to egg mixture and mix thoroughly. Fold in stiffly beaten egg whites and chill.

154

VANILLA CREME
Krem Waniliowy

2 cups sweet cream
¼ cup sugar
Vanilla bean or extract
5 egg yolks
2 T sugar
1 T gelatin

2 T cold water
1 cup whipping cream
½ cup Maraschino liqueur
1 T gelatin
½ cup warm water
1 T sugar

Mix cream with quarter cup of sugar, vanilla and bring to boiling point. Beat egg yolks with 2 tablespoons of sugar until thick, and add to cream mixture, stirring constantly. Do not boil. Dissolve 1 tablespoon of gelatin in cold water, heat in double boiler until smooth, and add to custard. Beat whipping cream with 1 tablespoon of sugar until thick. Add liqueur and 1 tablespoon of gelatin dissolved in warm water. Add to cooled custard, beat for 10 minutes and chill over night.

STRAWBERRY CREME
Krem Truskawkowy

2 cups strawberries
¾ cup powdered sugar
1½ T gelatin

¼ cup cold water
Juice of 1 lemon
1 cup whipping cream

Wash and hull berries. Mash and strain through sieve. Add lemon juice and sugar and stir until dissolved. Soften gelatin in cold water, place over hot water and steam until dissolved. Add to strawberries. When mixture starts to thicken fold in stiffly beaten cream. Pour into mold rinsed with cold water. Chill until set. Garnish with strawberries.

ALMOND CREME
Krem Migdałowy

½ lb. blanched almonds
2 T water
1 qt. sweet cream
1 cup sugar

2 T gelatin
¼ cup cold water
2 cups whipping cream
1 jigger rum

Pound almonds in mortar with a pestle until they are well crushed. At intervals add 2 tablespoons of water or more to prevent oil from separating in the almonds. Scald the cream and add the almond mass. Bring to boiling point but do not boil. Cool and strain through fine sieve. Add sugar, rum and gelatin dissolved in cold water. Beat until it begins to thicken. Then add the whipped cream and mix carefully and thoroughly. Chill.

155

CHOCOLATE CREME
Krem Czekoladowy

1 cup milk
Vanilla bean or extract
2 ozs. baking chocolate
1/2 cup sugar

3 egg yolks
1/2 T gelatin
2 T water

Melt chocolate in milk. Beat sugar with egg yolks until smooth and creamy. Add little by little to the hot milk, stirring constantly until it comes to the boiling point. Do not allow to boil. Add vanilla and gelatin dissolved in water. Cool, stirring vigorously at first and then from time to time to prevent crust from forming on top.

ORANGE CREME
Krem Pomarańczowy Wyśmienity

8 eggs, separated
Juice of 2 oranges
Juice of 1 lemon

1 cup sugar
1 T gelatin
2 T cold water

Pour lemon juice over sugar and beat until white, adding egg yolks one at a time. Add orange juice. Dissolve gelatin in cold water and stir over hot water until smooth. Add to egg yolks. Fold in stiffly beaten egg whites and pour into mould to chill. Serve with whipping cream and candied fruits.

CRANBERRY PUDDING
Kisiel z Żurawin Najsmaczniejszy

1 lb. cranberries
5 cups water
1/2 cup cornstarch
2 T cold water

1 1/2 cups sugar
3 whole cloves
1 small stick cinnamon

Cover cranberries with water and cook until tender. Press through sieve. Take only 1 cup of the liquid for this pudding. Add 4 cups of water to the cup of cranberry liquid. Add sugar, cloves and cinnamon and bring to boiling point. Make smooth paste of cornstarch with 2 tablespoons cold water and add to boiling cranberry sauce. Cook until thick and smooth. Remove spices and turn pudding into sugar-coated mold. When cold, serve with whipping cream.

GOOSEBERRY PUDDING
Kisiel z Soku Agrestowego

1 cup gooseberry juice
1 cup water
10 lumps sugar

6 T cornstarch
2 T water
1 cup white wine

Rub sugar lumps on skin of lemon to absorb lemon oil. Add water to juice and sugar. Bring to boiling point and thicken with cornstarch mixed with water. Add wine and stir until thick. Turn into sugar lined mold and cool.

156

APPLE NOODLE PUDDING
Pyszna Legumina z Makaronu

Egg noodles cut very thin   4 cups apple sauce
  (see page 28)   3 T butter
2 eggs   1/4 cup dry bread crumbs
1/2 t cinnamon

Make noodles, using 2 cups flour and 3 eggs. Cook in boiling salted water. Cool in colander under cold running water. Drain. Spread on a thin sheet and set in the oven to brown. Cook the apple sauce and make very sweet. Apple sauce should not be too thick. Mix noodles with eggs, cinnamon, butter and bread crumbs. In a buttered baking dish place alternate layers of noodle mixture and apples until all is used up. Sprinkle bread crumbs over the top and bake uncovered 25 minutes at 350°. Delicious with lemon sauce.

APPLE FRITTERS
Jabłka w Cieście

1/2 cup flour   1 egg white, stiffly beaten
1 T melted butter   1/2 cup beer
1/4 t salt   Apples, sugar, lemon juice
1 egg, beaten

Sift flour with salt. Cream butter, add egg and flour. Add beer gradually, stirring only until the mixture is smooth. Set in warm place for 1 to 2 hours to let the batter become light and foamy, then fold in the beaten egg white.

Peel large apples, remove cores. Cut in 1/4 inch slices and sprinkle with sugar and lemon juice. Let stand about an hour, moving them around so all apples will absorb the lemon juice. Dry the slices a little, dip in fritter batter and fry in deep hot fat until golden brown. Drain well. Put in hot serving dish and sprinkle with powdered sugar.

APRICOT OR PEACH COBBLER
Legumina z Moreli lub Brzoskwiń

12 large apricots or   1 cup powdered sugar
6 medium peaches   3 T granulated sugar
4 eggs, separated

Peel peaches, not apricots. Cut fruit in half and remove stones. Break stones and take out the seeds. Blanch them and chop fine, adding 3 tablespoons of sugar. Beat yolks with powdered sugar until thick. Add chopped seeds and mix well. Fold in egg whites stiffly beaten. On a buttered baking pan spread half of the batter. Cover with fruit and top with rest of batter. Bake in moderate oven for 30 minutes. Serve warm with thick cream.

Gruszki na wierzbie obiecywać.
To promise pears on a willow tree.

157

PLUM FLUFF
Śliwki w Pianie

2 lbs. Italian prunes
1 cup sugar
1 cup wine

4 egg whites
Sugar and vanilla

Bring sugar and wine to boiling point. Add plums and simmer until tender. Butter a fruit mold and fill with plum mixture. Beat egg whites until stiff. Flavor with sugar and vanilla to taste. Spread on top of plums and set in oven to brown. Serve hot.

CHERRY SOUFFLE
Suflet z Wiśni Surowych

2 cups bread cubes
½ cup sugar
¼ t cinnamon
Butter, size of an egg

Milk to soften bread
1 lb. pitted cherries
¼ cup chopped almonds
3 eggs, separated

Soften bread cubes with milk. Add sugar, cinnamon and butter. Add pitted cherries, almonds, and mix well. Add egg yolks, and last fold in egg whites. Butter and sugar a fruit mold. Pour mixture into mold and bake in 375° oven for 15 minutes. Serve at once.

RICE FOR DESSERTS
Ryż do Legumin

2½ cups milk, scalded
1 cup rice
6 T sugar
1 T butter

¼ t salt
Vanilla
3 egg yolks, slightly beaten

Wash rice in cold water, put in saucepan and cover well with water. Bring to a boil, turn off heat and let stand 5 minutes. Drain and bathe rice in cold water. Drain and return to pan and add milk, sugar, salt and vanilla. Bring to boiling point, add butter, cover pan and simmer very gently about half hour. (It is best to cook in double boiler about 45 minutes or until rice is done). Toss with a fork to separate the grains, then combine with egg yolks. Spread on a platter to cool.

158

CREAMY RICE PUDDING
Budyń z Ryżu

½ cup rice
½ t salt
1 t vanilla

½ cup sugar
5 cups milk
½ cup raisins (optional)

Bring to a boil 4 cups of milk, the salt and sugar. Wash rice in cold water, add to boiling milk. Simmer slowly for about 30 minutes or until rice is tender. Put rice in buttered baking dish, add remaining cup of cold milk, flavoring and the raisins. Bake at 400° for about half an hour or until the top browns slightly. Serve hot or cold with rich cream.

CEREAL PUDDING WITH RUM
Budyń z Kaszki z Arakiem

2½ cups milk
½ cup sugar
½ t salt
½ cup farina

½ t almond extract
2 T rum
2 eggs

Bring milk, sugar and salt to a brisk boil. Stir in the farina and cook for about 15 minutes. Remove from heat; add eggs, one at a time, beating each egg into the mixture carefully. Add flavoring and pour into mold. Chill for several hours. For serving, remove from mold, pour rum over the pudding, sprinkle with sugar and pour more rum over the pudding; set fire to the pudding as you carry it to the table.

BREAD PUDDING
Budyń z Chleba

Dark rye bread—one slice per person
Heavy raspberry or cherry syrup
Raisins
Whipped cream, sugar and vanilla

Saturate generously the desired quantity of dark coarse rye bread with the fruit syrup. Add about 1 tablespoon of raisins to each slice of bread. Mix well and let stand several hours. Cover thickly with whipped cream, sweetened and flavored with vanilla and serve.

Only the very dark rye bread may be used for best results and syrup should be "oozing" from the pudding.

CABINET PUDDING
Budyń z Pozostałego Placka lub Baby

Left-over coffee cake or cake
2 cups milk
Vanilla bean or extract
½ cup sugar
2 eggs

2 egg yolks
2 T raisins
Candied orange peel
½ cup fruit preserves
1 T lemon juice

In a deep mold spread a layer of the pastry broken into small

159

pieces. Then sprinkle candied orange peel and the fruit preserve or any other fruit you may have on hand over the pastry. Make custard by scalding milk and vanilla. Mix eggs and egg yolks with sugar and beat thoroughly. Add milk gradually. Strain. Pour custard over the top. Repeat layer, using all ingredients. Cover mold and set in a pan of hot water. Bake in moderate oven about 40 to 50 minutes or until set like custard. Serve with sweet cream.

MERINGUE
Meryngi

4 egg whites	1 cup whipping cream
1 cup sifted sugar	Sugar and rum
1 t cream of tartar	Mixed fruit

Beat egg whites until they hold up peaks. Add sugar gradually, beating egg whites after each addition. Bake in slow oven for one hour.

Whip cream until stiff. Add sugar and rum to taste. Spread on cooled meringue and top with mixed fruits such as pineapple, apples, prunes, pears, peaches, apricots.

ICE CREAM SAUCE
Sos Kremowy

1 pt. vanilla ice cream	2 T rum
1 egg, beaten	

Add the egg and rum to the vanilla ice cream. Beat well. Put into refrigerator trays to harden and keep until ready to use. Good for many desserts.

CHOCOLATE CHERRIES
Wiśnie w Czekoladzie

2 lbs. large, perfect black cherries	½ inch vanilla bean
3 cups sugar	1½ cups brandy to 1 cup syrup
1 cup water	Bittersweet chocolate

Combine sugar, water and vanilla bean and cook to fairly thick syrup. Cool slightly. Add brandy and mix well. Wash cherries and wipe carefully with cloth dipped in brandy, being careful not to break off stem. Place loosely in sterilized jars, stems up. Cover with syrup, seal. Store away until December.

Remove cherries and drain well. Melt chocolate over hot water. Dip cherries one by one, making sure that each is thoroughly coated and that the chocolate forms a seal around the stem. Put on waxed paper to harden. Store in tins, nesting them gently in strips of tissue paper. Serve at tea time or with after-dinner coffee.

Use delicious cherry brandy remaining in jars over vanilla ice cream.

MARZIPAN
Marcypan

1 lb. almonds   Flavoring (rose water)
1 lb. powdered sugar

Grind almonds very fine. Combine in saucepan with sugar and flavoring, cook until mixture leaves side of pan. Roll like pie crust. Cut in small heart shapes, lay on buttered paper and place in warm place to dry. Decorate with cherries or any other fruit.

RASPBERRY JUICE
Sok Malinowy

2 lbs. sugar   2 lbs. raspberries
1 cup **water**

Bring sugar and water to boiling point, add raspberries and continue boiling for three minutes. Cool. Strain through cloth and let drip clean. Boil syrup and fruit juice again for 15 minutes, skim and seal hot in jars or bottles. Excellent with tea or puddings.

CHRISTMAS "KUTIA"
Kutia Wigilijna

1 cup wheat   1 cup honey
2 cups water   2 cups water

Soak wheat for six hours. Cook in water until tender. Cook honey with water. Cool and serve with wheat. This dish is traditionally served in the southeastern provinces of Poland with other foods on Christmas Eve.

~~~~~~

CHRISTMAS HAY

Sweet Christmas-hay—More fragrant than the rose
That lights the thorn-bush on a summer hour,
And fairer than the lily, in repose
Lifting her chalice in an Easter-bower—
Nurtured to beauty by the scented rain
On banks that guide the roaring water's run,
The upland, meadow, hill, and rolling plain,
Windblown and ripened by the urgent sun!

Sweet Christmas-hay, my Polish childhood knew,
You cradle in your tangled wisps the white
Unleavened bread, and spread your fragrance through
The mystic silence of the sacred night . . .
While we remember how the Virgin smiled
Beside a hay-filled manger on her child.

                           —Victoria Janda

Walls of Space, 1945

CHRISTMAS

Christmas in Poland retains much of its story book fascination.

This holiday is preceded by a period of four weeks during which fast is observed on Wednesdays, Fridays and Saturdays. Strict fast is observed throughout the day before Christmas, and in the evening, the **Wilia** Supper is served. It is the most solemnly celebrated occasion and is so closely connected with family life, that members of the family who are away feel very deeply their absence from home. Polish housewives prepare for days in advance the traditional foods, beverages and decorations.

When the first star appears in the Eastern skies, the family gathers at the table for the **Wilia** Supper, a feast to commemorate the birth of the God Child. In farm homes, sheaves of grain, tied with colored ribbons, are placed in the corners of the room with a silent prayer for a good harvest in the next season. There is always a thin layer of hay under the white tablecloth in memory of the God Child in the manger. In every house in Poland, all members of the household, before sitting down to the table, break the traditional wafer, **Opłatek,** and exchange good wishes. The **Opłatek** is a thin unleavened wafer like the altar bread in the church, stamped with the figures of the God Child, the Blessed Mary, and the Holy Angels. It is known as the Bread of Love. The wafers are sent by mail to the absent members of the family.

The Supper itself differs from other evening meals in that the number of courses is fixed at seven, nine or eleven; and in no case must there be an odd number of people at the table. Otherwise, some of the feasters would not live to see another Christmas! A lighted candle in the window symbolizes the hope that the God Child, in the form of a stranger, may come to share the **Wilia** Supper, and an extra place is set at the table for the expectant guest. This belief stems from the ancient Polish adage, "Guest in the home is God in the home."

162

The **Wilia** seems very long to the children who are impatient for the lighted Christmas tree. Christmas trees are very popular in Poland. In the large houses in the cities they are placed on the floor or the table; in the villages they are hung from the ceiling, all decorated with apples, nuts, candies and many small toys made out of blown eggs, colored paper and straw. It is supposed that the gifts were brought by an angel, since their St. Nicholas had visited the children on December sixth. An old Christmas carol is sung and then the gifts are opened. More carols follow and there is great joy and merriment.

Polish carols, **Kolendy**, are very numerous and beautiful. They are sung at Midnight Mass, the **Pasterka** (Shepherds' Watch), and it is a popular belief in the villages that while the congregation is praying, peace descends on the snow-clad sleeping earth, and that during this holy night the humble companions of men, the domestic animals, assume voices; but only the innocent of heart may hear them.

Christmas Day is spent in rest, prayer and visits to various members of the family.

From Christmas Eve until Twelfth Night boys trudge from village to village with an illuminated star and a ranting King Herod among them, to sing carols. Sometimes they penetrate the towns in expectation of more generous gifts. In some districts the boys carry puppet shows called **szopki**. These are built like a little house with two towers, open in the front where a small crib is set and before which marionettes sing their dialogues. During the Christmas season the theaters give special Christmas performances.

On the feast of the Epiphany, the priest and the organist visit the homes, bless them and write over the doors the initials of the Three Wise Men (KMB) in the belief that this will spare them misfortune.

The Christmas season closes on February second, Candlemas Day. On that day people carry candles to church and have them blessed for use in their homes during storms, sickness and death.

Among the Poles, wherever they are, the most beloved and beautiful of all their traditional festivities is that of Christmas Eve. In the words of their forefathers, who called the Christmas Days, **Gody,** it is to them a time of good will, love, harmony, forgiveness, and peace.

SUGGESTED CHRISTMAS EVE SUPPERS

Seven Course

Herring and pickled mushrooms
Clear barszcz and mushroom **uszka**
Pike with horseradish sauce
Baked sauerkraut with yellow peas
Fried fish with lemon rings
Dried fruit compote
Pastries, coffee, nuts and candies.

Nine Course

Pickled herring and boiled potatoes
Mushroom soup
Pierogi
Baked lake trout
Baked sauerkraut with yellow peas
Fish in aspic and potato salad
Rice ring with creamed shrimp
Jellied compote
Pastries, coffee, nuts and candies

Eleven Course

Appetizers:
Pickled herring, individual salads, **pierożki**
  with mushrooms and browned butter
Creamed fish soup with dumplings
Pike fillet baked with cream
Baked sauerkraut and mushrooms
Pike in aspic
Cauliflower with crumb and butter topping
Fried fresh salmon and potatoes with tomato sauce
Prune compote
Poppy seed cake
Nut pudding
Pastries, coffee, nuts and candies.

164

STANLEY LEGUN

IN CONCLUSION

For a long time members of Polanie Club have felt the need for preserving in America some of the best Polish recipes. While there were Poles in the Jamestown colony, the Polish immigration movement did not reach its peak until after the partitions of Poland in the nineteenth century. This migration lasted until the restricting laws were passed in 1915. Therefore, the Poles belong to the later immigrants and as a result many good cooks who have come from Poland are still among us. On the shelves of the libraries are Polish cook books, yellowing with age, sent to the United States when exchange of thought between Poland and other countries was free.

TREASURED POLISH RECIPES for Americans is the result of research into these old precious cook books, invaluable help from good Polish cooks and the contribution of cherished recipes and cooperative help of all our members.

We have chosen recipes for foods available everywhere in America; yet we have kept every recipe in its original native tenor.

All recipes have been tested. We found many that directed the use of "enough flour to make a stiff dough" or "enough milk to make a pouring batter." Such recipes were carefully tried and the "unmeasured" ingredient was carefully measured and made part of the recipe in standard of measures common in America.

We are sincerely grateful to all who helped to assemble this book.

We hope the book will give our American cooks a new experience in preparing Polish foods and much pleasure and a real joy in eating them.

POLANIE CLUB
Irene Jasinski
Marie Sokolowski, Editors

Publications Committee: Josepha Contoski, Virginia Fitzsimons, Victoria Janda, Lucille Jasinski, Monica Krawczyk, Alina Polzak, Maria Smorczewska-Bullis.

RECIPE INDEX BY CHAPTERS

166

167

169